Robot Ecology and the Science Fiction Film

This book examines what is arguably the most important science fiction "meme," that of the robot, considering its centrality to science fiction (sf) film and the sf imagination from an "ecological" perspective that privileges the larger media environment of the robot. It focuses on three key characteristics usually considered in such ecological approaches: a meme's longevity or persistence over time, its fidelity or degree of similarity across various texts, and its fecundity or ability to inspire other developments. These three categories are then linked to a larger "robot ecology": the figure's function across different film genres, across different media, and in different areas of popular culture. This approach points toward a key question generated by the persistence of the robot in our media: the extent to which the human, constructed by various genetic, environmental, and cultural forces, has in the postmodern context increasingly come to seem as also a kind of technological fantasy, as another part of a thoroughly technological world. It is a question that is near the core of cinema as well, and one reason that film, science fiction, and their robotic progeny have all proven so important and fascinating to modern audiences.

J. P. Telotte is a professor of film and media at Georgia Tech. Co-editor of the journal *Post Script*, he has published widely on film and television with a special emphasis on science fiction. Among his recent publications are *The Essential Science Fiction Television Reader*, *Science Fiction Double Feature*, and *Science Fiction TV*.

T0347745

Routledge Focus on Film Studies

Robot Ecology and the Science Fiction Film

J. P. Telotte

Routledge
Taylor & Francis Group

NEW YORK AND LONDON

First published 2016
by Routledge
711 Third Avenue, New York, NY 10017

and by Routledge
2 Park Square, Milton Park, Abingdon, Oxon OX14 4RN

First issued in paperback 2018

Routledge is an imprint of the Taylor & Francis Group, an informa business

Library of Congress Cataloging-in-Publication Data
Names: Telotte, J. P., 1949–
Title: Robot ecology and the science fiction film / by J. P. Telotte.
Description: New York & London : Routledge, 2016. | Series: Routledge focus on film studies | Includes bibliographical references and index.
Identifiers: LCCN 2015042831 | ISBN 9781138649583 (hardback : alk. paper)
Subjects: LCSH: Science fiction films—History and criticism. | Robots in motion pictures.
Classification: LCC PN1995.9.S26 T465 2016 | DDC 791.43/615—dc23
LC record available at http://lccn.loc.gov/2015042831

ISBN 13: 978-1-138-59807-2 (pbk)
ISBN 13: 978-1-138-64958-3 (hbk)

Typeset in Times New Roman
by Apex CoVantage, LLC

Contents

Acknowledgments

Despite the slightness of this volume, many people have contributed significantly to its development and publication. Let me especially thank Sean Redmond and Leon Marvell whose collection *Endangering Science Fiction Film* gave me the impetus to re-examine the robot figure, and whose comments on my contribution to that collection influenced my work. Veronica Hollinger and the other editors at *Science Fiction Studies* contributed substantially to the development of Chapter 2, an early and shorter version of which appeared in that revered journal. At my home institution of Georgia Tech I benefitted from conversations with and support from a number of valued colleagues, among them John E. Browning, Angela Dalle Vacche, Carol Senf, Richard Utz, and Lisa Yaszek, while my Dean, Jacqueline Royster of the Ivan Allen College of Liberal Arts, provided critical support with a grant that allowed me to finish this volume in a timely manner. Finally, I want to thank the editorial team at Routledge for their encouragement of a book that I assumed would be very difficult to place, and also for their—as ever—efficient and professional work in pushing this work to completion and publication. In this group let me especially single out Simon Jacobs, Felisa Salvago-Keyes, Allie Simmons, Sarah Thomas, and Sheri Sipka, all of whom made my working with Routledge, once again, a great pleasure.

1   The Robot as Cultural Meme

Film and science fiction (sf) have a long-standing, practically historical, and certainly telling connection. From the earliest days of film, and long before the genre even acquired its proper name, filmmakers were creating sf-like texts: accounts of marvelous journeys such as Georges Melies' *A Trip to the Moon* (1902) and *The Impossible Voyage* (1904), futuristic visions like *The Last Man on Earth* (1924), and astounding inventions like those depicted in J. Stuart Blackton's robot short, *The Mechanical Statue and the Ingenious Servant* (1907), and Mack Sennett's *The Inventor's Secret* (1911).[1] Of course, many of these early titles simply remind us of the prior development of the sf imagination within the framework of a distinctly science and technology–inflected literature, illustrated most prominently by the work of Mary Shelley, Jules Verne, H. G. Wells, and even Edgar Allan Poe. But that kinship also owes much to the very nature of film. As an art form made possible by scientific and technological advances—that is, as a scientifically driven fiction—it initially developed in the context of what historian Tom Gunning has termed a "cinema of attractions" (63), that is, as texts built around—and thus reflecting—the amazing technical ability for image reproduction and fantastic illusion that was the early cinema's stock-in-trade. In the developing genre of sf, film simply found both a natural ally and a rich resource that it could readily mine for such attractions.

Our efforts to study that sf cinema, however, have often tripped over what, in the years since the genre's development, has become an increasingly knotty relationship—of film, sf literature, sf in popular culture, and more broadly, the sf imagination. Such efforts have especially been complicated by our disciplinary vantages, because those interested in and knowledgeable about sf in its literary and cultural artifact versions often have little or only passing concern with the cinema, whereas those invested and trained in cinema or television studies often pay little attention to the literature, theory, and the broader culture surrounding sf, save perhaps in instances when that material intersects with the large field of genre studies. Some of this disjunction is understandable, because the work of visual sf tends to be very different from the work of, for example, sf literature, whereas the broader interests of sf, or what I shall keep referring to here as the sf imagination, usually seem to bulk beyond the historical and theoretical concerns of film studies. In fact, even something as fundamental—and certainly a potential meeting ground—as one of sf's often-acknowledged core appeals—its ability to provide audiences with what Michele Pierson and others have termed an "aesthetic experience of wonder" (168)—seems to operate quite differently as we move across media or shift focus to different elements of popular culture.[2]

Figure 1.1 The mysterious metal man menaces Harry Houdini in *The Master Mystery* (1919). Octagon Films.

What I want to do here is explore a small portion of this tangled territory by slipping across some of the usual boundaries of study. In fact, my perspective might seem somewhat paradoxical, because it involves examining just a single image, that of the robot/android/cyborg/replicant, as it has taken hold in that sf imagination and found a particularly central place in our sf films. Because my own primary interest is in film studies, and because the image of the robot has resonated with such special power in our cinematic texts, I want to survey this territory primarily from that vantage. But doing so, as we shall see, also allows—or at least *invites*—us to consider a number of other elements implicated in the sf imagination's robotic vision—elements that together constitute what I would like to describe as a "robot ecology" of the sf film. Although grounded in the cinema, then, the following efforts to describe the broad outlines of that ecology will involve us in considering, or at least acknowledging, a variety of other components, including sf literature and theory; other cinematic genres; and other media forms, such as television, graphic arts, advertising, stage shows, toys, etc.—all of them components in that robot ecology, all of them helping to constitute in the popular imagination what has become one of the most important tropes in sf and arguably the most powerful image of the sf cinema. The hope is that by following the track of this artificial figure, we might find along this tangled path a productive way of considering some of the linked elements that have informed not only the development of the robot image, but also other components of our sf cinema, all of which together help constitute that sf imagination and the story it tells about the robot.

A primary reason for taking the robot as a stalking horse here is because it has attained a status that resonates not only with some of the key concerns of contemporary culture over the last century, but also, as I have already implied, with the very nature of film. Although the robot has, of course, given us a vehicle for exploring issues of gender, race, and a variety of forms of Otherness, and increasingly for asking questions about the very nature and meaning of life, this image of an artificial being, most commonly anthropomorphic in form, also invariably implicates the cinema's own and quite fundamental artificing of the human. For despite the common impression that film essentially *mirrors* the real, it is, as we well understand, always presenting even the human image through a process of various technological constructions as artifice: as something chemically reproduced on a film's emulsion (or rendered in pixels by a computer, the confusing potential for which we see explored in the 2002 film *S1mOne*); as visually fashioned from a combination of long, medium, and close-up shots, at times even cobbling together parts of *different* bodies through those different shots, as with Arnold Schwarzenegger's face and a younger actor's body in the recent *Terminator Genisys* (2015); and as enhanced by a mix of artificial lighting, color manipulations, prosthetic appliances, and various sorts of digital "enhancements," resulting in bodies—such as those rather spectacularly realized in the comic book adaptation *300* (2007)—that ultimately do not correspond to any we might encounter in the real world. Although some might simply suggest that this point means little, because most film actors are, after all, rather "robotic" themselves, that all film understandably trades in various sorts of illusion and reconstruction, or that all film bodies—not to mention our own imaginations—are invariably "cinematized" in one way or another, we would do well to note this dimension of the robot, this fundamental filmic correspondence. For it binds together at a most basic level the work of both sf and film, speaking directly to one of the sf genre's ultimate aims, while reminding us of ways in which the very medium always implicates a large part of that sf aim: the genre's consistent efforts to measure out, whether for today or tomorrow, the impact of science and technology on our humanity.

In this investigation, then, we are going to look through the lens provided by that robot figure in order to see a bit more deeply into the relationship between sf and the cinema—a relationship bound together by that sf imagination. This particular figure's longevity, dating from a time even predating the introduction of the term *robot*; its recurrent focus on certain conceptual issues, such as those of gender, class, and power; and its ability to conceptually develop or produce offspring, such as the various androids, cyborgs, and replicants found throughout our films today, attest to both the robot's place in and influence on the cultural imaginary—effects that have, in fact, allowed it to distribute meanings across a wide range of media texts and that thus reward our considering a sampling of those varied texts, describing, at least in part, what I term a robot ecology. But film's manifest fondness for this particular "attraction"—a fondness partially measured by the robot's appearance over the years in a broad array of films, including cartoons, live-action comedies, musicals, murder mysteries, and horror films, as well as our sf narratives—also suggests something of its medium's singular capacity for, as Francesco Casetti eloquently offers, "intercepting the impulses of twentieth-century modernity," guiding them "in a particular direction, regulating their intensity, combining them, tying them to certain patterns or exigencies . . . giving them a model against which the spectator could compare him or herself" (5). Consequently, we shall need to see the cinematic robot as more than simply a descendant of Mary Shelley's Frankenstein monster (1818), more than a technological evolution of something like the title figure of Edward S. Ellis' dime novel *The Steam Man of the Prairies* (1868), and more too than a holdover from or descendant of that early "cinema of attractions" of the 1890s to 1910s. It is, in fact, something of an image of film's own development, of what has been increasingly shown to be its own rather sf-ish nature.

I want to organize and explore this tangled relationship, as I have described it, not by surveying the robot in all its history and variety, but rather by looking systematically at certain dominant *types* of robots in order to better understand their implications for film, science fiction, and even contemporary culture. Consequently, I do not want to suggest that, despite a roughly chronological treatment, what follows is a history of either the robot or of sf film. In an earlier and rather traditional approach to this figure, I used the image of the artificial being in much this way, as a conventional diachronic measure, a way of focusing on particular achievements in the larger history of sf cinema and weaving those achievements together to form a roughly representative genre history. Given the lack at that time of a good history of the sf cinema, providing that sort of chronicle was my primary concern. To work up to that history, I began by observing how versions of this image of human artifice have been a part of Western culture from the time of the ancient Greeks to the present, an important touchstone in sf literature, particularly as it developed in the nineteenth and early twentieth centuries, and an almost constant presence in our sf films—indeed, one of sf cinema's most common semantic conventions found, as we have already noted, even in its earliest days. My belief was that because of this almost constant presence and the way it aligned the human figure with the powers of science and technology (as both the originator of those powers and, quite often, their "beneficiary"), the artificial being could help us chart the film genre's development or, more precisely, the various ways in which cinematic sf has evolved, while using the robot to address various key concerns, among them our cultural anxieties about the work of science and technology, our human concerns about the body, and especially in more recent years, its commonly gendered and racial identity, and even the changing nature of the technology-dependent art of film itself.

However, while that previous "robotic history," as I termed it, allowed for the *glimpsing* of various other implicated histories and suggested some intriguing links, it invariably came up short in several obvious ways. One was with accounting for how that artificial, robotic figure held on to our imaginations—and our films—sometimes for decades, before suddenly coming to seem rather quaint, rather like a nostalgic figure of film history, an aged but beloved performer/star, as it were. A second was with its seemingly easy ability to reach across genres and media, to become—and here I want to borrow a useful metaphor from the recent work of Henry Jenkins, Sam Ford, and Joshua Green—a kind of "spreadable" trope,[3] able to inhabit different parts of the media landscape, easily extending its sf character in a variety of directions and providing *meanings for* different sorts of audiences, including a non-sf audience. A third was with adequately explaining the relationships between one sort of robot "performance" and another, with talking about their particular connections rather than their function as chronological signposts in a larger generic/cinematic development. What I hope to do here is to address these, as well as several other concerns, not so much to revise that earlier history, but rather to provide in brief form some of the critical texture that it, as well as similar studies, lacks.

In order to do so, I want to frame this discussion in the fashion of a "robot ecology" (and thus as a supplement to that earlier "robotic history"). I use this term to indicate an examination of the cinematic robot not simply as a generic icon with a long pedigree, but rather to designate its relationship to other parts of its real and cinematic "environment," including literary and cultural components where those are most pertinent, elements that contribute to the larger sf imagination's ruminations on how science and technology affect our humanity. Some of these "other parts" include a rising tide of machine/technological consciousness throughout modern culture, a tide that has led some historians and theorists to describe sf as the fundamental literature of technical/industrial culture; the development of sf as a distinct genre, using its key tropes or icons in ever more sophisticated ways; and the gradual proliferation of computers, or "thinking machines," in our culture and in the world of entertainment. As Neil Postman, one of the leading figures in establishing this ecological perspective, has offered, the ecology of a thing or a medium "includes not only its physical characteristics and symbolic code," but also "the conditions in which we normally attend to" that subject, conditions that are typically "accepted as natural" (79), taken for granted as elements of the cultural air that we breathe, but that, as a result, often go almost unnoticed. Yet they are, as he argues, part of a complex system—much like the biological environment—that implicates and even requires from us certain ways of thinking about or responding to a subject, in this case the increasingly insistent figure of the robot. In fact, I would suggest that we take this notion of *required* thinking in a double sense, as suggesting not only how certain elements of our cultural ecology prompt us to think in certain ways, but also how those elements make it increasingly imperative that we give thought to them and their operation on us—a point I hope this short monograph can begin to advance.

To help us move from Postman's more general sense of the term to a more media-oriented approach, what follows relies heavily on Matthew Fuller's *Media Ecologies*, which, as his plural use of the term might suggest, looks at various mixtures and interactions of media and media systems. In fact, Fuller cautions from the start that the term ecology has been used "in a number of ways" and has consequently become rather "ambiguous . . . given its number of different uses" (2–3). For example, although Fuller employs it to describe the workings of pirate radio stations in the United Kingdom, he also applies the term to organize a discussion of different surveillance and crime reporting mechanisms. Another practitioner, Jane Bennett, uses the principle of ecology rather differently—but quite effectively—to "articulate a vibrant materiality" of inanimate objects that, she suggests, almost invisibly "runs alongside" the human realm (*Vibrant* viii). Drawing on these and other examples, I emphasize ecology's special ability to incorporate difference, to designate and examine what Fuller describes as "dynamic systems in which any one part is always multiply connected . . . and always variable, such that it can be regarded as a pattern rather than simply as an object" (4).

The focus of this study, as I earlier suggested, is itself multiple, keyed at times to particular robots in specific films or media texts, but more often concerned with robotic types or patterns as they have developed and persisted in the cultural consciousness—for example, in different genres (musicals, serials, science fiction, animation), in different media (not just film, but literature and television as well), and in different time periods (from the early twentieth century to the present). And because of those necessarily multiple connections (and multiple connections to multiple connections), what follows makes no claim to being an exhaustive analysis—*the* robot ecology. In this brief, demonstrative volume, we could not follow every cultural synapse that our robotic image might cause to fire within the sf imagination. So although we shall gloss over much of this figure's literary development, which has been treated elsewhere, we shall also draw into the discussion some particularly telling elements from the realms of popular culture—advertisements, journalistic accounts, toy lines—while omitting others, all in order to focus more precisely on the *patterns* noted earlier, especially on the visual appearances that help constitute its cinematic context. The study that follows simply offers—hopefully—a telling view of the dynamic sf and cinematic system in which the robotic figure has come to play such a central and allusive role.

Further following the method demonstrated by Fuller, Bennett, Susan Blackmore, and others, our ecological discussions of the robotic figure will be organized within a "memetic" scheme; that is, I want to consider the robot as a kind of cultural "meme" and thus draw upon the characteristics typically used to describe it. A meme is a term originated by evolutionary biologist Richard Dawkins, who offered it as a useful way of speaking about ideas or concepts in the same fashion that we have come to talk about genes and their biological functions (and one that, I want to suggest, might be equally useful for considering the nature of another gene near-rhyme, the genre). Explaining that parallel conception of gene and meme, Dawkins suggests that we think of the latter as a significant cultural concept that is subject to "cultural transmission," an analogous process, as he explains, "to genetic transmission in that . . . it can give rise to a form of evolution" (190). For Dawkins, as well as for others who have adopted this explanatory notion, the meme's greatest power lies in its status as a "replicator," something that can propagate itself, or various versions of itself, within or across minds and media, and in a practically evolutionary fashion, thereby helping to explain the process of cultural development—and perhaps, in another version of that evolutionary thrust with which Dawkins is most concerned, even something as basic as human survival (208), as we adopt and adapt certain ideas to help us cope with various environmental, social, and even ideological challenges to our individual and cultural well-being. This is a claim that, I should note from the start, I do not think is too ambitious to be made for the sf cinema.

Although the precise means of such memetic transmission remain open to speculation and explanation, proponents who have described this replicator activity commonly point to several key characteristics that mark the work of cultural memes, specifically, "longevity, fecundity, and copying-fidelity" (Dawkins 208). The first of these categories refers to the meme's strength, its ability to linger across time periods, or in the case of the cinematic robot, as it extends its popularity and impact across decades of films. "Fecundity" designates its apparent ability to produce permutations, slightly varied versions of itself, and versions that can, in turn, infect—or inflect—other texts and other media. Thus the robot might, in any period, assume slightly different shapes and display variations on a central theme, while it also points toward the appearance of more divergent robotic visions later on. The notion of "fidelity" indicates the meme's communication of a central idea, its ability to project an essential character. Although such an essentializing component might run counter to current critical fashion (which tends to find all notions of essence suspect or threatening), it seems important to recognize that there must be something fundamental to its robot-ness that this figure carries within it and, in its embodying of that concept, helps us to understand. Taken together, these characteristics offer a compelling explanation of the power that a cultural image such as the robot wields, as well as some insight into our own roles in the development of these images—or as Dawkins offers, they might begin to suggest how we, too, are "cultured as meme machines" (215), or, more accurately, as I would suggest, *as human media*, helping to convey the information bound up in such images.

These characteristics also give sense to what I have termed the "spreadable" nature of an image like the robot. For they can help to address some of those broad contextual matters that all too easily escape from many other approaches, such as my former historical/cultural reading of the sf cinema. For example, a particular robotic meme's longevity provides us with a measure of its ability to spread across various texts, genres, and media—and then rather rapidly to contract, disappear, or simply become a figure of nostalgia, still embraced or valued but as a kind of empty vessel or too-thin spread, important largely for what it *once* conveyed and now vaguely (or thinly), through its lingering traces, helps us recall. Its fidelity points to the inherent appeal of a certain robotic pattern, one more easily gauged by the faithful replication of its *primary* features across texts, genres, and media, or the slightness of alterations in its replications. The meme's fecundity places it in a larger historical context, one in which Dawkins' replicator activity comes to the fore, helping us see how one type of robot relates to another, in fact, how a meme like the robot participates in the hard work of cultural—and media—evolution by helping to generate an even more powerful or *meaning*ful image as its successor. By focusing attention on the robot's characteristic longevity, fidelity, and fecundity, then, we can draw on ecological analysis' basic assumption that, as Fuller offers, "it is one of the powers of art or of invention . . . to cross the planned relations of dimensionality—the modes or dynamics that *properly* form or make sensible an object or process" (2), thereby adding more texture to our historical accounting, spreading it across many sorts of texts or platforms, drawing in elements that our disciplinary *discipline* might otherwise push to the sidelines of investigation or simply ignore altogether.

For the purposes of this particular investigation, our focus will be on three primary forms that the robotic meme has taken in the course of cinematic history. These are, as subsequent chapters will note, by no means the only forms of the robot, but they are those that have demonstrated a most powerful and telling persistence or longevity in our sf cinema, while also most clearly extending their influence beyond the film genre's normal boundaries. One is the purely mechanical figure, often referred to as the tin-can or sheet-metal robot. A descendant of Ellis' Steam Man constructed of boilerplate, this sort of robot appeared in film after film, almost unchanged, from the early 1930s to the mid-1950s. Perhaps most familiar from the 1935 sf/Western/musical serial *The Phantom Empire*, it is also a close kin to the Tin Woodsman of the very non–science fictional *The Wizard of Oz* (1939)—and thus to the various other "constructed" metal figures of L. Frank Baum's literary Oz, that is, not only the Tin Woodsman, but also such figures as Captain Fyter, Chopfyt, Tik-Tok, and the Iron Giant. A second is the complex humanoid robot with an electronic brain, linked to the various sorts of "positronic" robots most famously chronicled in Isaac Asimov's *I, Robot* (1950) stories and typified by Robby the Robot of *Forbidden Planet* (1956). After its introduction in this iconic film, Robby would reappear in movies, television, advertising, and on toy shelves throughout the following two decades; it would inspire a variety of imitators; and it would linger into the present where it has remained available—in a reminder of that nostalgic shift noted earlier—as a museum exhibit, but also as a kind of adult toy, a full-scale, complete-in-every-detail mock-up figure, created for and sold largely to movie memorabilia collectors. The third type is the human-seeming—and sometimes morphing—cyborg or android, featured not for the first time but certainly most influentially in Ridley Scott's *Blade Runner* (1982) and, of course, in its source novel, Philip K. Dick's *Do Androids Dream of Electric Sheep?* (1968), as well as in the various *Alien* and *Terminator* films, multiple television series, theme parks and fairs (there labeled as "audioanimatronics"), and various contemporary journalistic discussions about the cultural and psychological impact of such cybernetic figures. Although these three variations on the robot neither encompass the full history of the figure in sf cinema nor sketch the very multiple forms it has taken across modern—and postmodern—culture, each has for a time dominated our sense of the artificial being, effectively imprinting it on our cinematic imaginings until supplanted by another, more "moving"—that is, similarly compelling and meaningful—image that has then held sway in our psyches, suggesting both the hopes and the fears that culturally we—and the cinema—have invested in this figure. By considering the powerful persistence of these three figural forms, I believe we might better understand the appeal and significance of the robotic image and, to some extent, even that of sf cinema itself.

Of course, there are many other robot types we could consider—all across our mediascape—most of them discussed in detail or at least touched on in my previous study and elsewhere.[4] So before we turn to our primary types, we might just sketch a very brief historical context for the cinema's robot imaginings, focusing our attention on the implications of some of these varied forms the robot has taken. Proto-robot stories, often about mechanical wind-up figures or steam-driven machines—and often preceding film's emergence—abound and include such diverse works as E.T.A. Hoffmann's story "The Sandman" (1816); the ballet *Coppelia* (1870) partly based on Hoffmann's work; August Villiers de l'Isle-Adam's "android" novel *The Future Eve* (1886); a variety of dime novels that closely imitate Ellis' *The Steam Man of the Prairies*;[5] a number of Baum's Oz stories, as we have noted; the early British film comedy *The Mysterious Mechanical Toy* (1903) and the J. Stuart Blackton short cited earlier, *The Mechanical Statue and the Ingenious Servant* (1907); Mack Sennett's Keystone comedy *A Clever Dummy* (1917); and even the Fleischer brothers' cartoon *Mechanical Doll* (aka *The Dresden Doll*, 1922). These and similar works in the late nineteenth and early twentieth centuries largely depict simple machines, at times qualified by an element of fantasy or even (in the case of *The Future Eve*) mysticism. But these simple devices in roughly human form easily speak to issues of labor and machine power that have continued to haunt and taunt modern technological society.

There is also an obvious element of mystification behind an interesting and scantly noted entertainment parallel of relatively short but consistent form that anticipates most of the film developments to be discussed. From the early 1900s and lingering well into the 1930s, a popular and recurrent attraction in vaudeville theater, British music halls, amusement parks, and other live presentations was the fake mechanical being, or automaton—typically a wax-masked actor or costumed character, frequently gendered as female, thereby injecting a telling male-over-female power relationship into the presentation, and usually accompanied by a presenter, or "inventor," who would display, comment upon, and in some cases invite audience

Figure 1.2 Displaying the inner workings of Enigmarelle, an early "robot" act.

interaction with the machine-like figure, or "invention," being exhibited for their amazement. Among these popular figures were Phroso the Mechanical Doll (circa 1902), who would later be featured in a film by Alf Collins, *The Mysterious Mechanical Toy* (1903); Enigmarelle (1904), "a cleverly-constructed figure which apparently walks and writes automatically," as a *Scientific American* article offered ("Clever" 46); the "Mysterious Fontinelle" (1911), theatrically billed as "The Marvel of Late Invention"; and William Mackford's Rose-Marie, a blond-haired and probably Coppelia-inspired dancing robot (1925). Although accounts of these presentations can be found in a wide range of publications, ranging from the serious *Scientific American* to the British humor magazine *Punch*, these were essentially fake robot acts, designed to entertain audiences with their illusion of controlled, mechanical operations, usually abetted by a variety of highly visible and audible effects—machine-like sounds, exposed metallic parts, elaborate electrical control boxes, connecting cables—while posters and print advertisements often posed the audience-challenging and essentialist question, "What Is It?"[6]

The key attraction to most of these figures—the live entertainment ones noted earlier, as well as those in literature and early film—was their fundamental ability to blur the sense of difference between human and machine. And that ability was repeatedly underscored in various ways, such as when Mackford would dance with and even kiss his female robot, or by characters' tendencies to fall in love with or be charmed by such mechanical creations, as Koko the Clown sadly does in the Fleischer *Mechanical Doll* before his beloved literally dissolves on the film. However, these acts and narratives ultimately offer little exploration of the nature and cultural implications of the robot. They are, rather, simply presented as remarkable inventions—or fake inventions—important as demonstrations of technology's power to astonish, as early signposts for a significant direction that the sf imagination would take, and as embodiments of what Adam Roberts has termed a certain "Will-to-Power" bound up in a variety of such efforts that have in common an imitation of the human and a seeming desire to control others through the power of technology (174).

But even many later visions of the robot, especially figures that stand in stark contrast to such generally anthropomorphic images, have also tended to avoid direct examinations of the robot's nature. These later types—often small, curiously shaped, and gifted with a limited on-board intelligence—have instead emphasized the robot's function as a kind of "sidekick," pet, or helpmate. Among these rather diverse figures, we might note the three dwarfish "drones" of *Silent Running* (1972)—Huey, Dewey, and Louie—designed to help tend giant greenhouses in space; the squat, tracked Omega of the East German–Polish space travel film *Der Schweigende Stern (Silent Star*, 1960), used to scout the dangerous surface of Venus; the floating repair and sanitation robots V.I.N.CENT and Old B.O.B. of Disney's *The Black Hole* (1979, and subsequent comic book series), who do repairs, store information, and provide protection for their human companions; Twiki, the small "ambuquad" robot who assists Buck Rogers in the television series *Buck Rogers in the 25th Century* (1979–81); and especially a figure like R2-D2 of the many *Star Wars* films and their offshoots, a squat, multipurpose unit, resembling a waste can, that in almost every film manages a moment of heroic action and at times even seems capable of human-like emotions, albeit emotions that are practically always subordinate to a servile obedience.

Although often servant-like, these and many similar nonanthropomorphic robots are the sort that have often been described as "loveable" types—a description that effectively marks their basic *narrative* function. They are loveable partly because they are presented as evoking fondness from other characters in their narratives, and thus suggesting the sort of relationships that help support the workings of classical film narrative. Yet they are also loveable because they do *not* really resemble the human and so tend to function as a kind of technological "pet"—a status that interpolates an element of difference or class system into the narratives, while also allowing them to evade an uncanny response from viewers. Not an obvious focus of that "power" motif that Roberts identifies, such figures have as one of their key functions the mirroring or underscoring of the relationships of the

Figure 1.3 A "pet" robot, Omega, from the Polish–East German *Silent Star* (1960). DEFA Studio.

surrounding human characters, as they emphasize the importance of those relationships while also deflecting concern about the robot's own nature.

Most other robotic figures seem to speak more directly—and with increasing complexity—to our hopes and fears for this sort of creation. For example, after the appearance of Karel Capek's landmark play *R. U. R.* (*Rossum's Universal Robots*) and its introduction of the term "robot" in 1920, a more complex figure began to surface in the popular imagination through early sf literature, several live-action feature films, and various noncinematic appearances. Both *R. U. R.* and Fritz Lang's epic sf film *Metropolis* (1927) do dwell on the human *seeming* of their created figures. The former emphasizes that although its robots are actually organic creations and look deceptively human, they have little of the human within them. Thus one of the robot designers proudly explains to a group of visitors their simple design: "Not much in it, but everything in flawless order" (9). In the latter work the gleaming metal robot developed by the scientist Rotwang is given a sympathetic human appearance, that of Maria, a beautiful young woman and leader of the people, expressly to deceive the dystopian city's workers and help in their repression by Metropolis' leader. Appearance, both of these texts suggest, is important to their robotic story.

But more significantly, both play and film develop a specific function of the robot, giving it a place in cultural discussions of the period about the role of labor. Thus *R. U. R.* depicts a world in which the transfer of human work to machines is eagerly embraced by society, although that transfer eventually leads to a robot revolt and heralds the end of mankind. *Metropolis* places the robot at the center of a plot to control unruly laborers and

Figure 1.4 The introduction of the robot Maria in *Metropolis* (1927). UFA.

eventually do away with the worker underclass, a plot that fails and finally brings the city's leader into negotiations with the workers. Both texts stand as stark warnings against easy technological solutions to the rising tide of labor problems and worker alienation, particularly in a world where technology has prompted many of those problems, given the Fordist practices of the early Machine Age.

While framing these same concerns with labor and technology in a broadly comic way, a number of animated cartoons of the 1920s and 1930s would also take up this issue of creating mechanical workers. Ub Iwerks' *Techno-Cracked* (1933), for example, shows Flip the Frog reading an article in *Unpopular Mechanics* entitled "Technocracy: Why Be a Slave." Inspired by the piece, he follows its instructions for building a robot to take over his household chores; that creation, however, then destroys much of the house. Similarly, Columbia's *Technoracket* (1933) has the character Scrappy, inspired by reading a like newspaper piece, build a group of robots to do all of the labor on his farm, although this development then puts the farm workers and even the farm animals out of a job. And in *Bosko's Mechanical Man* (1933) Warner Brothers' Bosko also tinkers together a robot out of scrap to help with his chores, but the robot proves to have a mind of its own and becomes more menace than machine assistant. These and a number of other efforts in the period manage to avoid the more serious dimensions of the labor issues by rendering their problems not as societal ones, but rather as individual missteps, as comic mistakes for which their cartoon figures pay a simple comic price.

Figure 1.5 Scrappy's robots rebel and make him pay a price for their creation in *Technoracket* (1933). Columbia.

Notwithstanding these warnings, both serious and comic in nature, as Lisa Nocks describes, a number of such mechanical figures were being introduced at trade shows and world fairs from the late 1920s throughout the 1930s. Among the many such exhibits were Eric the Gomshall Robot, which appeared at the London meeting of the Society of Model Engineers in 1928; Alpha the Robot of the 1935 California Pacific International Exposition; the Budapest robot from the Hungarian International Fair of 1937; and, probably the most famous, Elektro the Motoman of the 1939–40 New York World's Fair.[7] All, as Nocks notes, seemed to demonstrate the same point— the robot's great labor-saving potential—while also "amusing the crowds as they showed off the latest in electromechanical engineering" (56). As the 1940 industrial short *Leave It to Roll-Oh* produced for the New York World's Fair promised housewives of the period, once robots like the titular Roll-Oh are in place, "Your domestic problems are completely solved"— and implicitly a life of leisure awaits.

A later generation of such figures would prove more complex—and more challenging—as their machinic chassis were increasingly linked to other technological developments in the postwar period, while often being sundered from the Depression-fueled questions surrounding labor. Along with Eric Frank Russell's Jay Score stories, Isaac Asimov's *I, Robot* tales, originally published in various pulp magazines between 1940 and 1950, especially helped usher in this new vision of the robot: as a creation that would have a mind of its own (provided by its "positronic brain"), and thus potentially an inner *life* of its own as well, thereby suggesting that it would need to be controlled in some way to prevent it from possibly usurping humanity's central place in the world—the consequence previously forecast by Capek's *R. U. R.* The result was Asimov's formulation of what has come to be known as the Three Laws of Robotics, a safety feature programmed into his stories' robots and, afterward, a common regulation figured, usually in slightly different formulations, into a host of cinematic and other media robots. As articulated in Asimov's 1942 short story "Runaround," those laws, "built most deeply into a robot's positronic brain" (40), are as follows:

> One, a robot may not injure a human being or, through inaction, allow a human being to come to harm.
> Two, . . . a robot must obey the orders given to it by human beings, except where such orders would conflict with the First Law.
> And three, a robot must protect its own existence as long as such protection does not conflict with the First or Second Laws. (41)

Later, Asimov would add another provision, a "Zeroth Law," as it has become known, stipulating that robots may not harm *humanity*—a kind of overriding condition that clarifies the larger function of these rules. As one of Asimov's characters reminds us, these rules ultimately have their source in "the essential guiding principles of a good many of the world's ethical systems" (158). Thus the safeguards they provide function as a kind of technical Ten Commandments for robots, imposing a mechanical morality in their dealings with humans, while also ensuring, at least for a time—and in an interesting commentary on the shifting vision of religion and its function in society—their lower place in a new hierarchy of intelligent beings.

As we have already noted—and as we shall later explore in depth— *Forbidden Planet*'s Robby would most prominently usher into the cinema, as well as much of popular culture, just such a mind-ful robot. But other and similar figures bound by Asimov's laws have subsequently surfaced throughout popular culture in television series such as *Doctor Who* ("The Robots of Death," 1977), *Star Trek: The Next Generation* (see especially the character of Data in "The Measure of a Man," 1989), the animated *The Simpsons* ("Simpsorama," 2014) and *Futurama* (1999–2003, 2010–13); in other films, including *Aliens* (1986), *Robocop* (1987), and *Bicentennial Man* (1999); and even in video games like *Robot City* (1995), *Halo* (2001), and *Portal 2* (2011). Yet more important than the acknowledgement of those laws is the foregrounding, especially in works obviously influenced by Robby (as we shall see in Chapter 3 of this volume), of the hard moral choices that such rules frequently impose on both man and machine. In one of the more famous Soviet-era sf films, *Planeta Bur* (*Planet of Storms*, 1962), for instance, the robot John—who very closely resembles Robby— introduces himself to his human companions on a mission to Venus by explaining, "I am a free-thinking machine." Subsequently, while on Venus, John and two human cosmonauts become trapped by a deadly lava flow, and because he has been programmed to protect humans, John begins to carry them through the danger, even though it means partially immersing himself in the molten rock. However, when he begins to melt, his "self-protection" circuitry automatically kicks in, and he announces that he will have to drop his human burdens to save himself. At this point his companions must choose to shut down that circuitry and thus sacrifice their "free-thinking" metal companion, or be left to die themselves in the lava stream. The result is a difficult moral decision, framed by John's seemingly conscious status and by all of his past efforts to help them selflessly through the many dangers of their mission.

Because we do so often judge, even make difficult moral decisions, on the basis of appearance, and because John, Robby, and others in this vein are such clunky and clumsy approximations of the human form, thinking anthropomorphs of this sort typically prove a bit less challenging, allowing for somewhat easier or more obvious moral decisions, than a later generation of robotic creations that look just like us. Thus it is those later developments, of figures that underscore how practically indistinguishable the robot/android/cyborg/replicant figure might ultimately be from the human, that, as we might expect, most directly implicate and interrogate our sense of self, while also exposing issues of gender and race that are commonly linked to appearance. As an example, we might recall the situation facing *Blade Runner*'s detective protagonist Rick Deckard. Pressed into the job of tracking down a group of escaped "replicants" and "retiring"—or killing—them, including several women, Deckard sees how challenging it can be to deal with such artificial beings: testing their reality, fighting with them, separating his emotions from the difficult, life-taking task at hand. Although he manages to dispatch several of this group, he also falls in love with Rachael, a replicant whom he initially thought to be human, and he must finally fight for his life against the leader of these artificial beings, Roy Batty, who at one point taunts him, noting, "I thought you were supposed to be good. Aren't you the *good* man?" It is the sort of provocative question that increasingly seems to emanate from films in which robots appear to be practically indistinguishable from the human. Even more so than the artificial beings of other, earlier robot texts, such figures have simply proved very effective for embodying and exposing a broad range of cultural issues linked to our sense of self—especially issues of cultural prejudice and valuation—while also posing disturbing questions about human behavior and our attitudes towards difference or Otherness, all issues that ultimately reflect on and help constitute what we might commonly think of as our own human goodness.

As testimony to the imperative and indeed pervasive nature of such questions, to their obvious importance in a period when we are already fashioning figures that look disturbingly like ourselves and as we seem to be nearing a point of robotic "singularity"—that is, a time when such artificial intelligences will catch up with or surpass the human and be lodged in bodies remarkably like our own—*Blade Runner* and many similar texts have easily spread these sorts of interrogations across a wide variety of media. The success of the film *Blade Runner* resulted in the re-release of author Philip K. Dick's original novel, *Do Androids Dream of Electric Sheep?*, and inspired a comic book adaptation in 1982, several video games, various novel sequels by other authors, and a planned film sequel. Across a similarly broad media range *The Terminator* (1984, 1991, 2003, 2009, 2015) film series has given rise to a television offshoot *Terminator: The Sarah Connor Chronicles* (2008–09), a video game, several comic book series, action figures, and a popular Universal Studios theme park attraction, *Terminator 2–3D*, all of them exploring this issue of human likeness, emphasizing that our ability to confront and sort out the issues surrounding such robotic figures might represent a kind of life-or-death imperative for contemporary culture—one most memorably articulated in *Terminator 2* (1991) when the human Sarah Connor, under attack by one Terminator figure, is, to her shock, suddenly offered help by another who asks her to trust him, simply stating, "Come with me if you want to live."

These and similar texts found across the media landscape repeatedly suggest that such human-seeming figures do represent an important and compelling challenge to us, particularly as they signal a bridge between the postmodern world in which we live and what some today refer to as our *posthuman* state. In a variety of ways the postmodern emphases on skepticism, on the elusiveness of any sort of objective knowledge, on the disappearance of traditional values, including religion, and especially on the problematic nature of our representational systems (resulting in what is generally termed the problem of the real) do readily dovetail with a posthuman sensibility. For the latter term signals a variety of current cultural efforts to look beyond traditional conceptions of the human and of human nature, in the process opening the door to other possibilities for and definitions of the human, even other notions—for example, extra-biological—of future human evolution. One such notion is, obviously, technologically based, and is represented by the pairing of ever more sophisticated artificial (robot-like) bodies with electronic brains that are the equivalent of or more powerful than human ones. Seen in the context of this linkage, the human-seeming robot becomes not simply a threat, our possible replacement or "termination," but, in all of its variety that we are exploring—including hybrid versions of the human, equipped with various sorts of prostheses or on-board memory/intelligence enhancements—a potential expansion of our measure, of what the "human" might ultimately mean. In fact, this new type may well be what we need to embrace if, as a species facing critical environmental challenges, even the possibility of species extinction, we do indeed "want to live." It is precisely the point made by the cyborg character Major Kusanagi in Mamoru Oshii's celebrated anime *Ghost in the Shell* (1995). When her partner Ishikawa asks why he, a human, was assigned to work with a cyborg and their part-cyborg partner Batou, she explains that their very differences make them effective, in fact, more so than a team of all humans or all cyborgs: "overspecialize and you breed in weakness; it's slow death."

But that notion of teamwork and potential kinship speaks to more than just the appealing, at times spectacular, and perhaps even necessary visions that our sf films and other media have typically generated. The robot is, as we began by noting, also part of a special dimension of the sf film experience. As various commentators have noted, the genre is simply one of the most self-conscious of forms. Nodding in this direction, Annette Kuhn points out how the sf cinema has consistently been characterized by a "mobilization of the visual"—by its emphasis on a plethora of technical devices for seeing and measuring, by the representation of what such devices "see" (readouts, holograms, surveillance tapes, digital images), as well as by a measure of sheer visual spectacle—all of which readily call to mind "the processes through which films produce their meanings" (6). In this reflexive respect sf suggests a kinship to such other film genres as the musical or the show business biopic, although the "performance" with which sf is centrally concerned is that of science and technology, the same science and technology that have made film possible and that allow us not just—as one of the fathers of sf, H. G. Wells, once suggested about film—to experiment with the idea of time travel, but to engage in all sorts of flights of fantasy, including the future of the human, and to better undertake the sort of "thought experiments" that many see as the very raison d'etre of the genre.

We might well think of the robot as simply one such "performance" that has proven particularly crucial in the evolving relationship between sf, film, and the sf imagination, while also helping in a very specific way to extend this generic self-consciousness we have noted. As several of its early appearances remind us, this figure is one that has persisted from the earliest days of film and, in fact, gained increasing resonance as we have moved into that posthuman era where—across the entire media landscape—we seem practically *compelled* to speculate about what it means to be human, especially when science and technology place before us various lures, such as an increasing array of replacement parts that might extend our lives; possibilities for genetic selection to ensure stronger, taller, more beautiful, and generally more capable offspring; and all sorts of technological augmentations to mind and body that could enhance or prolong the "human" experience. But the robot's persistent performance implicates more than just the nature of sf or even of sf cinema.

In his phenomenological study of film, Francesco Casetti notes a double thrust to all cinema that, I would suggest, repeatedly echoes in all of these robotic depictions and speculations. In one capacity, through its reflections and reconstructions of the human, film offers us a practically unavoidable mirror; as Casetti says, "on the screen, in spite of everything, we see what we have become" (85). At the same time, it foregrounds—and asks us to consider—the cinema's "new ways of looking at the world," ways that, he offers, "we can make our own" (85) as we seek to better understand both world and self. Of course, that reflection of the self and the reflexive turn of the mechanism are equally challenging, requiring that we not simply immerse ourselves in the fanciful products of our machinery, that we not, as Casetti says, "become puppets called to act a part that is a pale 'metaphor' of the self" (84), or that we become, as cultural critic Paul Virilio puts it, "mediatized" or "cinematized" (*Vision* 59), simply submerged in a world that has become a kind of extended movie set. Together these dual thrusts help recall the complex possibilities that all film holds out for us—possibilities that are more easily activated in the sf genre and brought more fully to the foreground with the imagery (or self-imagery) of robots. In a world dominated by science and its technological products, in a world that almost requires that we see through—that is, by means of—those same technological products, we also have to find ways of seeing them and perhaps seeing *through* or *beyond* them.

The film robot, as well as the broad ecology in which it exists, can help us in such tasks, even prompt the development of a new sort of ethics, such as Jane Bennett sees possible if we can just recognize our relationship to a "vibrant" and "vital materiality" (*Vibrant* 14) that is our world. In its dominant forms—those forms that the following chapters will examine in some detail—the robot serves as an important viewing device, much like film itself. It allows us to see ourselves in those compelling images that have persisted over time, reflecting how such technological fantasies—or technologies of fantasy, such as film itself—speak to the self and what they say about the self. At the same time, this figure helps us to see *through* those same fantasies or technologies to better understand how they work on us and what makes them so compelling. Moreover, with these levels of better vision, of better understanding, of what we might just call science fictional imagining, the robot in all of its ecological extensions poses another question for our consideration, namely, the extent to which the human, constructed by various genetic, environmental, and cultural forces, has in the postmodern context increasingly come to seem as also a kind of technological fantasy, part and parcel of a thoroughly technological world. It is a question, we might suspect, that is very near the core of cinema as well, and one reason that film, sf, and their robotic progeny have all proven so fascinating and manifestly important to us.

Notes

1 I draw these simple descriptions of basic sf texts from noted sf historian Edward James, who has identified three types of tales that have largely dominated the genre or, as he puts it, "determined membership" in it: "the extraordinary voyage," "the tale of the future," and "the tale of science" (13).

2 Some elements of that difference in treatment are discussed in Telotte and Duchovnay's *Science Fiction Film and Television: Across the Screens*. See especially the Introduction to that volume.

3 See Jenkins et al.'s *Spreadable Media* and its explanation of how the most successful media texts work in what has become a "convergence culture." Their argument, that the most successful companies "are those that listen to, care about, and ultimately speak to the needs and wants of their audiences" (xii),

might easily be extended in a historical/theoretical fashion to describe the most successful tropes for addressing those same "needs and wants."

4 In addition to my *Replications*, other useful studies of the robot image include John Cohen's *Human Robots in Myth and Science* (1967), Harry M. Geduld and Ronald Gottesman's *Robots, Robots, Robots* (1978), Barbara Krasnoff's *Robots: Reel to Real* (1982), Per Schelde's *Androids, Humanoids, and Other Science Fiction Monsters* (1993), and Lisa Nocks' *The Robot* (2008).

5 For discussion of the various "steam man" stories and their place in sf history, see Roberts' *The History of Science Fiction*, pp. 173–74, and Landon's *Science Fiction After 1900*, pp. 43–45.

6 Paul St. Pierre briefly discusses this automaton type, suggesting that it be seen "within the taxonomy of the living statue," a popular music hall entertainment of the late nineteenth century. Its primary distinction, as he notes, is that the "act involved deliberate machine-like movement," and thus played upon the period's rising fascination with machine culture (218). The "What Is It?" query is actually the title for a brief photographic essay on "Phroso the Wonderful Mechanical Doll" in *The Sketch* magazine on the occasion of its/his performance at the London Hippodrome theater in 1902.

7 A useful source for tracing out the appearances of both real and fake robots is Reuben Hoggett's Cyberneticzoo.com.

2 The Empire's New Robots

All objects have a poetics; they make the world and take part in it, and at the same time, synthesize, block, or make possible other worlds.
—Matthew Fuller, *Media Ecologies* (1–2)

Visitors to the Autry National Center and Museum of the American West may be surprised by a rather curious exhibit, a metal and pressed cardboard "robot head mask," as it is labeled, acquired by the museum from the famous Western Costume Company as part of Western's "Star Collection Auction."[1] Hardly a typical icon of the Western genre, this headpiece is apparently all that remains of the many "tin can" type robots that appeared in Gene Autry's first film, Mascot Studio's *The Phantom Empire* (1935), a serial that famously cobbled together a new and unlikely combination of

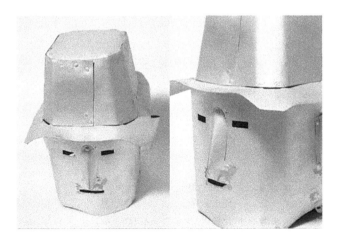

Figure 2.1 Robot mask used in *The Phantom Empire* (1935). Mascot Pictures.

Western, musical, and science fictional elements. Although the rather crude, expressionless figure this flimsy remnant evokes does little to suggest the sort of menacing robots that had previously populated the early sf cinema, creatures like the murderous metal man of *The Master Mystery* (1919), the seductive mechanical Maria from Fritz Lang's *Metropolis* (1927), or the giant monsters of Andre Deed's *The Mechanical Man* (1921)—all figures that dramatically brought to life early Machine Age anxieties about industrial culture—*The Phantom Empire*'s simple, stiff-legged, and boxy tin men were a fairly new but soon to be familiar type of the 1930s and 1940s, as well as a common element of the sf genre's "poetics," then and now. Moreover, their persistence in the cultural imaginary would "make possible" a host of subsequent robotic visions, and in that endurance, as part of what Matthew Fuller evocatively terms a "media ecology" (4), they help to remind us of some of the economic and cultural imperatives that have shaped our sf films, in both their most hopeful and most anxious forms.

I want to focus on this figure partly to demonstrate how useful that notion of ecology can be as an analytical tool for considering the work of film genres, but also to consider how such a potentially menacing—and hardly human-seeming—figure did for some time prove both attractive and compelling—both in our culture and as a component of a just-developing cinematic sf. As Fuller observes, our media are all embedded in a "dynamic interrelation of processes and objects, beings and things, patterns and matter" (2)—a relationship that underlies what Henry Jenkins has evocatively termed "media convergence" (3), and one that can have the effect of amplifying an image or pattern's power, extending its reach across genres and media platforms, and helping it to persist over time. As we noted in the introduction, Richard Dawkins' notion of "memes," those basic units of cultural information and even change, may account for how certain images, including certain robotic images, work across a variety of media texts, in effect forming links that help generate the sort of "media convergence" that has become a familiar marker of contemporary culture. However, because Jenkins is largely concerned with the *fact* of such convergence and, even more so, with its larger implications for our cultural trajectory, he gives little attention to the specific mechanisms implicated in that process. Rather, he simply refers to the "flow of content" (2), explaining how the "circulation of media content . . . across different media systems, competing media economies, and national borders" can eventuate in that "convergence" effect (3) he has so influentially described.

Fuller's media focus might be seen as building on Jenkins' observations by mapping out some of the key characteristics—or conduits—of that "flow," particularly as he pursues those three important memetic traits of fecundity, fidelity, and longevity, or what we might inversely describe as a meme's persistence over time, its relative consistency in form, and its ability to inspire other, related possibilities—similar yet altered images or narrative patterns that retain some of the original's significance or power. Considering such properties can add an effective dimension to more traditional genre studies, providing a dynamic context within which we might view, for example, the semantic and syntactic components influentially articulated by Rick Altman (680) in his study of genre mechanisms. These categories do so not only by describing a pattern of cross-genre "reach" or influence—thereby potentially broadening the genre "canon," "supertext," or "genericity" in much the way that Altman had earlier called for (689–90)—but also by helping to map out what he terms important "historical considerations" (686) that govern the workings of those semantic and syntactic elements, particularly as their *longevity* wanes while their *fecundity* continues to work, producing new variations on a characteristic image or pattern—variations that respond more effectively to changing cultural circumstance.

In this chapter I want to consider how this approach might help advance our thinking about media sf by focusing on the robot as it found a relatively consistent form in late Machine Age film culture, persisted in that form for several decades, and then, through shifts in meaning and/or function, made possible other conceptualizations of the robot. Specifically, this chapter focuses its attention on one curious and surprisingly cross-generic form this figure took in the 1930s–1950s period, as suggested by that Autry museum exhibit. For *The Phantom Empire*'s rather essentialist robots, the clanking, wobbly, sheet-metal creations emblematic of that film's advanced underground civilization of Murania (an early version of the cinematic sf utopia) begin to tell an interesting and suitably—for our purposes—limited story of a robot ecology. They are obviously easily identifiable, thanks especially to their peculiar metal top hats, and can help us trace how such figures found their shape, why they lingered on our screens and in our imaginations, and to some extent what the empire of cinematic robots—early and late—has meant to our sf films and especially to what was, during the time encompassed by this robot's longevity, an emerging sf culture.

In this particular early case, we can see in those popular robots a new turn, not so much a warning about this figure's potential danger, as a film like *Metropolis* had already so effectively sounded with its robotic Maria who brings an entire world to near collapse, but a dream of late Machine Age culture about a possible marriage between humanity and its manifestly powerful technological creations, one that ultimately suggests how we might begin to remake our world and even ourselves. However, it was a dream that would never quite see the sort of fruition envisioned in that film, and one that would undergo crucial changes, thanks largely to the impact of

World War II, which rechanneled many of the era's technological advances, while also lending them a new aura of menace, much as had, for a brief time, the mechanized slaughter of the previous World War. These robots' traces, though, would linger, phantom-like, mocking the technological promise of that between-wars era, one described by Richard Guy Wilson as the notion that "a whole new culture . . . could be built as readily as the machine" (23). I want to focus attention on this particular robotic image in part because of a very literal "marriage" in which it was early on involved, one that almost incidentally underscores its place in a larger technological ecology of the era. In this period machines of every stripe were, for a time, seen not as the sort of dangerous creations that would soon be realized in the war, and not even as simple semantic markers of a developing sf imagination, but as contributors to and signs of an efficient and emerging technological utopia wherein they might become key human supports or helpmates.[2]

The Autry museum's exhibit notwithstanding, the Empire's new robots were not quite so new. For this tin can type had already appeared in several unlikely places. One, as the introduction briefly noted, is in American cartoons of this period. Studios such as the Fleischer Brothers, Ub Iwerks, Columbia, Universal, and Disney all produced cartoons featuring versions of the tin can robots that look remarkably similar, although they often take on different characters. For example, Universal's Oswald the Lucky Rabbit vehicle *The Mechanical Man* (1932) offers a menacing robot created by a mad scientist, whereas in Disney's *Mickey's Mechanical Man* (1933) Mickey Mouse himself tinkers together a boxing robot that helps him win a match against a giant ape, "The Kongo Killer." Both Iwerks' *Techno-Cracked* and Columbia's *Technoracket* (both 1933) offer robots designed to do human labor, but in both cases these creations go out of control and, through their very power, do more damage than work. The Fleischer Brothers' *The Robot* (1932) and Columbia's *Man of Tin* (1940) similarly feature boxing robots, albeit robots that their creators—Bimbo in the former and Scrappy in the latter—must go inside in order to control. All look to be made of riveted metal or boilerplate, are vaguely anthropomorphic in shape, and prove either difficult or impossible to control, with those issues of control typically producing the main gags of the cartoons. However, the Disney, Fleischer, and Columbia robots, once properly controlled, prove to be useful human (or mouse or dog) helpers, even champions, effective tools for tapping into and succeeding in the new technological world.

A second and even more unlikely generic appearance of this figure, in fact, precisely the same robot as we find in *The Phantom Empire*, is in the Joan Crawford MGM musical *Dancing Lady* (1933), which also marked the first major screen appearance of another icon of the period, the very unmechanical yet immensely energetic star Fred Astaire. A variety of stills, rather

Figure 2.2 Joan Crawford surprised by a robot admirer in *Dancing Lady* (1933). MGM.

easily found online and ascribed to the film, show Crawford (as the character Janie Barlow) interacting in some intriguing ways with a number of these robots. Pointing up the film's pre–Production Code status, one image depicts six metal men working at various tasks, while another peeks around a corner and into showgirl Crawford's dressing room, obviously surprising her as she sits in her underwear. In several others, one of the tin men has removed his "head," revealing a handsome young man (or machine-man) inside that metalware who admires Crawford, still just slightly clothed in her shimmering, silken underwear, but now also modeling a bridal veil and long train. Additional images show a fully clothed Crawford standing hand in hand with her human-headed robot, as they are apparently being married by a clergyman with smiling witnesses in attendance. I call attention to these "found" images because even though they have been identified by those who post them, by captions on some of the stills, and by several historians as originating in *Dancing Lady*, extant prints of the film show no trace of this robotic surprise encounter, engagement, and wedding, as we might describe the image sequence,[3] contemporary reviews do not cite this rather striking and certainly unusual human–robot encounter, and Crawford biographies make no mention of this strange sf element in an otherwise conventional musical film.[4]

However, the group of images does seem quite appropriate to *Dancing Lady*, in part to its general plot trajectory, but especially to its large-scale, multiscene climactic sequence "That's the Rhythm of the Day." In this final and lengthy musical set piece, a number of old women, stooped figures wearing long black dresses of an earlier era, are ushered into a series of shops and salons where they are reclothed and physically transformed by the workings of various wonders of modern science—machines and chemicals—into attractive and active young women. Put through a kind of modern human assembly line, they have been rejuvenated, literally transformed into young "dancing ladies," as if they were themselves machines—or robots—that could be mechanically recharged and put in tune to the fast-paced rhythms of the day, rhythms that they then demonstrate in an elaborate dance routine. Moreover, the sequence echoes the larger thrust of the narrative, wherein Crawford, the eponymous "dancing lady," wins the heart of the cold, business-like—or machinic—producer played by Clark Gable and is, as a result, herself transformed from a struggling chorus girl into a luminous Broadway star.

Given the lack of contemporary commentary, we can probably assume that this strange phantom scene—a robotic encounter, revelation, and marriage to a machine-man—was simply cut before the film's premiere, especially because the larger musical sequence we have described was already, as Mordaunt Hall styled it, a "lavishly staged spectacle" that would have been "better suited to the Yale Bowl or Chicago's Soldier Field" than to any theater (Hall). In any case, its surprising origin in *Dancing Lady* seems confirmed by the fact that the same revealing image of Crawford in her underwear and wearing the bridal train, as well as an encounter with one of the robots, shows up in various other media representations of the film: on several posters, lobby cards, and even newspaper advertisements for the film.

Moreover, those robot images seem to have a telling and what might even be termed a persistent pedigree. The costume designer for *Dancing Lady* was MGM's famous lead designer of the period Adrian, who would later in the decade be responsible for another and far more famous tin can figure, the robotic Tin Woodsman of *The Wizard of Oz* (1939). So was this rather avant-garde designer, typically assigned to projects involving extravagant, high fashion, or ultra-modern costumes, responsible for an sf image that would linger for decades in the movies? Although there is no documentation of his work on the robot costume, Adrian biographer Richard Adkins notes that early versions of the Tin Woodsman costume closely recall the images from *Dancing Lady* and seem to confirm one of the designer's signature practices: his tendency to "recycle common design themes throughout his films,"[5] in this case, as he combined the general form of the *Dancing Lady* robots with some touches drawn from the John Denslow illustrations for Frank L. Baum's original *Oz* books and then altered both to better allow

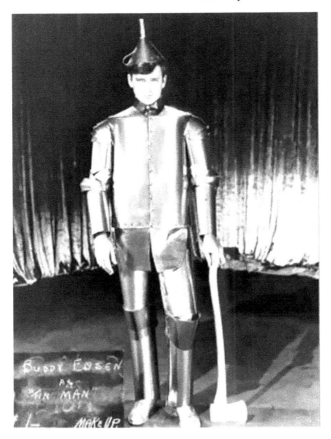

Figure 2.3 Costume by Adrian. The first design for the Tin Woodsman of *The Wizard of Oz* (1939). MGM.

for the singing and dancing required of the Tin Woodsman role in the 1939 film. That suggestive robot image's cross-media and cross-genre persistence simply stands as one trace of this early robot figure's complex ecology, of a sort that Jane Bennett, in describing another ecological pattern, has fittingly termed "an intricate dance" between seemingly disparate elements (31) of the cinematic world.

More than just traces of a pedigree, though, these ecological connections suggest a particular attitude that was becoming attached to the era's robots—one that markedly differentiates these figures from some of the monstrous projections that had initially marked their appearance in films. For with this sort of romantic contextualization, even fitting the robot within a world of song and dance, we can make out an effort to give a human face to Machine Age technology and potential, and to celebrate the hoped-for marriage between human and machine—or "humanity and nonhumanity," as Bennett puts it (31)—that, in keeping with the period's ethos, seemed poised to transform modern life. At the same time, the generic links here point to an interesting blurring of lines between the lived modern world and sf particularly—and suggestively—modeled in that cross-genre pairing of working-girl Crawford in her shimmering silken underwear with the "handsome" robot in its/his equally shimmering metalware.[6]

With this foundation for our robot ecology, we can further follow this trace across genres—and indeed across media, because the *Dancing Lady* images exist only as the various advertisements, production stills, and promotional shots described earlier and persisting on the Web—to the relatively well-known cross-genre effort, the sf-Western-musical *The Phantom Empire*. There we find not only the same robots, but also an illustration of how, as Fuller puts it, such "media elements possess ontogenic capacities as well as being constitutively embedded in particular contexts" (22–23). Thus the larger pattern we glimpse in the *Dancing Lady* outtakes, that suggested narrative of surprise, demystification, even humanization, and then marriage to the machine, points us toward a similar pattern in the later Gene Autry serial with its encounters between surface men and another, more elaborate vision of the Machine Age and technological culture embodied in that film's futuristic world of Murania—a context no less spectacular in costume and conception (or even music) than *Dancing Lady*'s elaborate "Rhythm of the Day" finale. With those same robots—or, to be more precise, robot costumes—being employed in the serial, we might well assume that these metal figures in their fecundity brought some of that same story— and perhaps even a hint of MGM "class"—with them.

When Mascot Pictures, a Poverty Row studio specializing in B-Westerns and serials, decided to try its hand at sf—at this time still a relatively obscure part of the genre landscape—it apparently chose not to create its own robots. With a characteristic eye to saving money—that is, an economic dimension of the media ecology we have been describing—the studio simply acquired a number of the tin can guises from the movie costume supplier Western Costume Company, which had either produced them for or acquired them from MGM. Along with some elaborate model work to represent Murania, a disintegrating ray that ultimately proves Murania's undoing, and a plot revolving around secret radium deposits, this robotic figure, this technological meme complete with its polished sheet-metal surfaces, roughly anthropomorphic contours, and slow, stiff-legged gait, would prove one of the film's key generic indicators, helping to anchor its other, incongruous generic elements—of both the Western and the musical—more firmly in the science fictional, while also providing a dose of what Michelle Pierson terms the "aesthetic experience of wonder" that has always been one of the genre's fundamental appeals (168). Moreover, these robots would invariably show up in *The Phantom Empire*'s own print advertisements—its various posters, lobby cards, and publicity stills—with that strange "top hat" headpiece intact, adding to its multiply allusive character: recalling the elaborately costumed musical world of *Dancing Lady* with its "fancy dress" robots, evoking the cowboy hats worn by Gene Autry and his companions, and even hinting of the robot's rather domesticated (i.e., properly dressed) status in this film and perhaps its suitability for other domestic contexts.

In fact, that status might be seen as another trace of the ecology we are noting. For Murania's robots, with their top hats and stark facial features that suggest their own almost surprised look, are neither threatening nor cunning after the fashion of those early cinematic ancestors we noted in *The Master Mystery*, *The Mechanical Man*, or *Metropolis*. They are, rather, part of its generic background, simple fixtures in an advanced technological world. When we first see one in *Phantom Empire*, there is certainly a moment of surprise for the audience as the science fictional rears its head because most of the serial's action up to that point has revolved around the typical icons of the Western—a ranch, horses, six-guns, even a stagecoach, all elements to be expected in one of Mascot's specialty B-Westerns or serials. But that initial surprise—or "sense of wonder"—is also tempered by the robot's actions, for the first one that appears in *Phantom Empire* is just turning a crank to open a door onto the surface world. The scene depicts the robot as little more than a laborer, much like those workers glimpsed in the first *Dancing Lady* image,[7] although as we later learn, it is a laborer with a machine's superior strength and endurance. Thus this and the other robots we encounter throughout the narrative lift things, work on assembly lines, carry loads, or, thanks to their infrared vision, serve as sentries at various doors and gates. And all of these mundane duties are repeatedly noted in the course of the serial's twelve episodes, as the robots become both wondrous representations of a desired world of the future—one in which, as Queen Tika of Murania proudly notes, "mechanical men do all the labor"—*and* commonplace figures, typically unheeded by Murania's citizens, as if they were the products of a marriage between humans and machines that has already, and quite successfully, taken place in this futuristic realm.

Of course, thanks to the uncanny nature that typically attaches to such figures,[8] these robots do retain a certain disconcerting effect, much like what we see when Crawford is startled by one of the working robots peering into her dressing room. And an element of that effect lingers when in *Phantom Empire* we see them carrying large metal beams that, the film demonstrates, no human can lift, or when Gene Autry is nearly killed when he falls

Figure 2.4 The Phantom Empire's robots: easily controlled by buttons and knobs (1935). Mascot Pictures.

onto a moving assembly line and a robot worker, acting in its mechanical and repetitive ways—much like a modern-day assembly-line robot—fails to heed his presence and almost applies a welding torch to his head, just before, in typical cliff-hanger fashion, his friends yank him away in the nick of time. But the serial repeatedly works to demystify or drain these figures of that uncanny or potentially disconcerting aura, allowing us to see *them*, as it were, in their underwear—or with their hats off. At one point Autry's sidekicks Pete and Oscar come upon a jumble of parts, including an array of motors and gears, from robots that have been partially disassembled, and Pete, after observing that they contain "wheels like a clock," adds with comic surprise, "Why, they're not alive at all!" Later, Autry's young ward Betsy, startled at seeing such figures for the first time, asks, "How do those things work?", and his other ward, the older and scientifically inclined Frankie, matter of factly explains: "Why, there's machinery inside, just like a clock, and they've got radios in their head, and there's a fellow at the central station that turns dials and things and tells them where to go and what to do." And indeed, that is exactly what we see in the course of the narrative. Easily controlled by "dials and things," turned on or off via buttons on their chests or by remote control, these robots are finally not very frightening, just human-sized, clockwork figures that people can manipulate, good assembly-line workers in the sort of Fordist economy that for the 1930s apparently extended from the United States on the surface to the underground and highly evolved world of Murania, 20,000 feet below.

Later still, we see a variation of *Dancing Lady*'s attempt to give a human face to these robots, as they become little more than costumes for Pete and Oscar. In their comic efforts at trying to rescue Gene from the Muranians, Autry's sidekicks find themselves chased by the empire's soldiers, so they duck into a room full of robots and hide among them. In a turn that comments on the nature of these metal figures—and that would later be echoed in Woody Allen's comedy *Sleeper* (1973) when he, too, evades pursuers by posing as a robot—Oscar and Pete empty out the clockwork-like mechanisms inside two of the robots and slip on the metalware, including headgear, literally becoming robot men, in the process recalling Crawford's robotic suitor (as well as such cartoon characters as Bimbo and Scrappy). In fact, Pete and Oscar prove so indistinguishable from the real robots that they manage to knock out, one by one, the Muranian soldiers who are searching for them, and from there they proceed to rescue Gene, where they then take off their headpieces, again miming Crawford's human/robotic hybrid and surprising Gene.

In her discussion of *The Phantom Empire*, Cynthia Miller describes this scene as just a comic interlude in the serial's larger adventure plot, as "the two imposters shift the roles of the robots from those of emotionless menaces to clumsy vaudevillians, drawing in the audience as collaborators in the comedic routine" (73). And indeed, when demystified in this way, in fact, when worn like suits, Murania's mechanical men do seem a bit comic, reminding us of Henri Bergson's famous description of the comic as "something mechanical encrusted on the living" (49), and perhaps better explaining their repeated appearances in the cartoons of this period. But as we have seen, that Bergsonian "shift" was not simply a bit of comic punctuation, but also part of their "story," an element of the memetic buzz attached to these tin can figures, as well as a hint of their promise. This ability to "inhabit" the robot reminds us of how easy it was in this period to be both taken aback by and accommodated to the latest technology, in effect, to be wed to a technology that was, after all, not so alien from us, that for the most part seemed harmless, and that might easily be controlled "by dials and things," wielded by a purposeful human manager, and, in some cases, even clumsy sidekicks.

However, when Mascot merged with Monogram Pictures and several other small companies to form Republic Pictures late in 1935, that ecology began to evolve. Slightly bigger budgets and a growing cultural interest in sf, partly fueled by such popular comic strips as *Buck Rogers* (1929) and *Flash Gordon* (1934), would result in many more films with robots, as well as slightly more elaborate robots to fill those roles: robots that retained many features of the Empire's, that even followed some of the patterns already described, but also ones that demonstrated their "fecundity" or possibility for development (114), even for embodying a new sensibility, especially for suggesting an element of danger that would increasingly attach to powerful technology in the years leading up to World War II.

The first step in this development would be *Undersea Kingdom*, Republic's second serial, released just a year after *Phantom Empire*. It largely follows the same plot as the Gene Autry film, with its hero, naval officer Ray "Crash" Corrigan (played, after the pattern of Autry in *Phantom Empire*, by Ray "Crash" Corrigan), discovering an advanced underground—or more precisely, underocean—civilization, in this case the legendary city of Atlantis, preserved in a geological bubble and evolved along different lines than the surface world. Here, too, robots become key semantic signifiers or marks of "wonder" for this futuristic realm, although they also assume a larger role in the action and manifest a slightly different character—one that is consistent with an evidently growing cultural ambivalence toward the technological in this pre-war era. Although retaining some of the memes of the Empire's robots, particularly the general tin can/sheet-metal form, awkward movements, and machinic power, these Volkite robots, as they are named, would prove something other than tireless workers or sentries. Not as sleek, gleaming, or attractive as their forebears and only slightly anthropomorphic, they more resemble industrial water heaters; they lack separate heads—never mind the tin hats—there are rivets visible across their bodies, and piping resembling water tubing or antennae runs from crown to shoulders. In place of shiny, metal appendages, they have flexible tubular

Figure 2.5 The dangerous Volkite robots of *Undersea Kingdom* (1936). Republic Pictures.

arms and legs, large steel claws rather than metal hands and fingers, and they are often shown carrying ray guns. More soldiers than nondescript laborers, they restore some of the robot's uncanny effect, rendering it as more menacing, a characteristic in keeping with its ultimate plot role as part of a mechanized army that is being developed by the Atlantian ruler Unga Khan to help him conquer the surface world—and one too that must have resonated with a rising tide of militarism and technological menace that was then being witnessed in various parts of the world.

And yet several memes from the Volkites' *Phantom Empire* kin persist, suggesting how that element of fecundity might work hand in hand with the image's near-fidelity to its previous form. For even with their altered look, these robots too are eventually demystified, prove susceptible to human habitation and control, and at least hold out a promise of servile status—of a profitable human "marriage" to the technology. Late in the serial, for example, Crash Corrigan and Professor Norton's son Billy, much like Pete and Oscar, take apart and examine a disabled robot. As Crash pulls out a chunk of gears and wires, young Billy asks with that same demystifying satisfaction observed in *Phantom Empire*, "They're just machinery, aren't they?"— simple enough for a child, a sidekick, or even a Machine Age moviegoer to comprehend. Crash then uses the emptied-out Volkite as a disguise, getting inside of its metalwork so that he can penetrate the Atlantian control tower, rescue Professor Norton, and then disable the tower's armaments before this destructive technology can be unleashed on the surface world.

With the threat of Atlantis vanquished, the serial concludes on a customary reassuring note, as we see Professor Norton dismantling and studying another of the Volkite robots that has been salvaged from that futuristic world. As he explains to Crash and Billy, he hopes to learn the "secret" to its control, and once that key is discovered, he announces, "all mankind will be relieved of the drudgery of physical labor"—thus allowing for the sort of hopeful relationship to the technological suggested by *Phantom Empire*. With that repetition of the robot costuming, with that rendering of the threat effectively understood and controlled by man, and with that promise to fully transform the Volkites into a miraculous labor-saving device that we could culturally embrace, *Undersea Kingdom* restores the ecology of the tin can robot, although it has obviously "made possible . . . other worlds," as Fuller would say, including more threatening ones, by surfacing a dangerous ontological potential that was also implicit in that form.

In fact, that development, the transformation of the humanly controlled and human-serving device into a potential menace, would mark most of the subsequent appearances of these metalwork figures in a host of Republic's pictures for more than a decade thereafter. With only a minor alteration— for example, eliminating the antennae-like piping—a Volkite robot would become the central attraction of the studio's *Mysterious Doctor Satan* (1940), a serial focused on the aptly named Dr. Satan's own efforts at world domination through machine technology. Tellingly billed as "Dr. Satan's Man of Steel" in the title of one chapter, the robot would demonstrate a frightening strength and deadly power, while in episode after episode, as William C. Cline notes, Dr. Satan continued his research into discovering an effective "means of controlling the machine from a distance" (49). But although the robot would be captured and in one scene have its own insides dismantled, inspected, and analyzed, just as in each of the other films we have discussed, it would never prove quite understandable, and that crucial element of control or accommodation, the ability to fully harness its startling power for labor or other useful purposes—which also forms the central plot concern for Columbia's later *The Monster and the Ape* (1945)—would spectacularly and quite tellingly fail here when, in the serial's final episode, Dr. Satan is himself killed when his mechanical creation runs amok.

But in typical serial economy, that water heater design, along with its now-menacing aspect, would persist in a host of other Republic productions, including *Zombies of the Stratosphere* (1952), later edited into the feature release *Satan's Satellites* (1958), and the combination serial/television series *Commando Cody: Sky Marshal of the Universe* (1953, 1955). In fact, the title of episode seven of *Commando Cody*, "Robot Monster from Mars," clearly underscores how the robot's function would become altered as work gives way to menace, and the humanly designed, and relatively easily understood, figure becomes instead an alien-controlled, alien-sourced creation, embodying not the promise but rather the very real threat that had increasingly become attached to all sorts of advanced technology in the immediate postwar era and that would eventually be illustrated in a host of succeeding cinematic robot types throughout the 1950s. Although still resembling a metal water heater or large tin can, the robot had become a figure quite beyond human habitation or control, not something we might give a human face to—or sing and dance with—but as alien and as unpredictable as a man from Mars—or a zombie, a monster, even a satanic creation—and something that, along with the other threatening Martian technologies of the *Commando Cody* serial, would have to be overcome by other sorts of human advances—and science fictional memes—such as Cody's backpack rocket, spaceship, and related inventions.

Yet those tin can robots, in fact, the very same ones left over from *Dancing Lady* and *The Phantom Empire*, lingered on the cinematic back lots to make a final appearance, further underscoring the changed character we have described: hardly laborers, they appear as menacing figures, elements of an alien task force bent on destroying the Earth. In 1951 Columbia Pictures, in an effort to capitalize on the highly popular—and notoriously economical—Dumont television series *Captain Video and His Video Rangers*,[9] would produce the fifteen-episode *Captain Video, Master of the Stratosphere* for theatrical release. In bringing the well-known cheap chic of *Captain Video* to the big screen, Columbia, too, probably for its own reasons of production economy, would draw on those well-used metal and top-hatted men from Western Costume, but, in an effort to insert them into a more contemporary Cold War context, the narrative would frame them differently in a way that spoke to the sense of technological menace with which people of that era daily lived and which a host of other robot-involved films of the period—among them, *The Monster and the Ape, The Day the Earth Stood Still* (1951), *Gog* (1954), and *Tobor the Great* (1954)—would readily evoke.

With scant alteration to their appearance, the *Captain Video* serial presents these tin cans as the "latest invention" of the evil alien leader Vultura, who simply describes them as his "electronic men"—one of many menacing devices he is developing on the distant planet Atoma as part of his plot to conquer the galaxy. Sent to Earth as a leading force in his invasion plans, two of the robots sabotage a chemical plant and knock out Captain Video's assistant, the Video Ranger. However, because they are so slow moving, clumsy—thanks to those same stovepipe arms and legs—and subject to the turning of "dials and things" from such a great distance away, they are simply overcome. In fact, Captain Video's own well-known *electronic* (as distinct from machinic) arsenal, many of the devices here carried in a seemingly bottomless bag of such tricks attached to his belt, prove far more uncanny and powerful than these by-now-dated bits of Depression-era metalwork. Using a variety of his own inventions that clearly reference the postwar world rather than the Machine Age—devices such as the supersonic detector, which amplifies sounds at great distances; the opticon scillometer, which allows one to see through objects; and the atomic disintegrator rifle, which blasts matter into tiny particles[10]—Captain Video rather easily defeats Vultura at every turn, whereas those lumbering "electronic men" simply disappear after two episodes in favor of Vultura's new assistant, the aptly named Dr. Tobor ("robot" spelled backwards), who has his own array of competing inventions and whose person already forecasts a new generation of robots, one that shares much with the human. At this point in history, as these screen villains bluster about very real threats, such as advanced rockets, hydrogen bombs, sabotaging the climate, and even dislodging the planet from its orbit, the top-hatted robots simply seem dated, neither surprising nor menacing, and not the sort of technology to which we might wish to be wedded, especially given the far more wondrously imaginative—electronic and atomic—alternatives offered by the ever-inventive Captain Video and the many similar space opera heroes of the 1950s.

Appropriately, just as *The Phantom Empire*, with its improbable combination of sf, Western, and musical elements was beginning to be seen in the new context of camp sensibility in the 1950s,[11] the Empire's once (almost) new robots had come to seem almost laughable in their impotence in this, their last screen appearance. They are neither frightening nor emblematic of core Machine Age values like efficiency, regularity, and power, as the films discussed here illustrate, and their potential as helpmates seems to have given way to darker possibilities, ones repeatedly linked to an inability to control such figures. And yet their influence—and longevity—is worth considering. Drawing together the Mascot film's robots and various other sf components, Jon Tuska argues that

> had there been no *Phantom Empire*, there may well have been no *Flash Gordon* from Universal in 1936 . . . or *Buck Rogers* from the same studio in 1939. . . . There for sure would have been no *Undersea Kingdom* from Republic in 1936 . . . nor would science fiction have become so much a staple of serial production for the next fifteen years (160).

Although that assessment probably overstates the case—because it ignores literary and comic sf, while obviously overlooking *Dancing Lady*'s almost spiritual contribution to this ecological system—the film's robots certainly tell a story of influence in their "replicator activity," as Fuller terms it (111), with their image repeating, persisting over an extended period, and displaying a potential for development—albeit a development that, in the Cold War era of atomic weapons, rocketry, sleek jet fighters, and international tensions, would eventually require major transformation. There was, after all, so much other and more powerful technology that we had to learn to control, lest we find ourselves culturally in the same bind as that mysterious Dr. Satan—destroyed by our own devices. But these figures also served a useful conservative function, for in the course of their replication, they managed to disguise or blunt some of the very real danger that had always been implicit in the robot concept, especially its subversive ability to foreground and interrogate the nature of human labor in modern technological society, or even to raise questions about gender and work, because these figures are never gendered, never presented as anything other than *things*. For a time, they simply translated those sorts of potentially explosive social issues into a concern with how we used—or misused—our machinic tools, as embodied in these simple tin can forms.

Of course, in that postwar era robots did not disappear from our films, although, as the next chapter will describe, the figure would find many alternative translations. Gort of *The Day the Earth Stood Still* (1951), the eponymous Robot Monster of *Robot Monster* (1953), and especially Robby the

Robot of *Forbidden Planet* (1956), all very different in shape and capabilities, would shift focus from those machinic issues of power and efficiency to other, more pressing ones. As we shall see, issues of control, of alien influence, and of robotic brains—concerns already rife in the fast-developing sf literature—would quickly come into sharp focus. In fact, Robby would achieve a similar status as a kind of robotic meme through his own longevity, appearing in a host of films and television programs over the following two decades, being imitated in a television show like *Lost in Space* (1965–68) and, through his linkage of cinematic sf with its literary kin, reinforcing the growing supertext of sf by helping to familiarize audiences with Isaac Asimov's famous Laws of Robotics, controls expressly intended to contain the implicit dangers of the robotic by ensuring that such manifestly powerful figures could not hurt, only efficiently and without question serve their human creators.[12]

But the Empire's not-quite-new robots had an amazing persistence in the cultural imaginary. These tinware figures that were surprising yet also surprisingly understandable, that were strong yet easily ordered about, that could be worn like a suit of new clothes in a way that suggested our far-from-secret desire to embrace or join with the seductive new world of science and technology—its metalwork as attractive to the 1930s as Joan Crawford's silk underwear—continued to dance through our early science fiction films. In the process they provide us a glimpse of how that imaginary depended on a complex ecology: one that involves the economy of special effects, such as robot "costumes" that could be handed across studios and

Figure 2.6 Elektro the Motoman greets the crowd in the Westinghouse Pavilion at the 1939 New York World's Fair.

even film genres; the persistence of certain themes, such as those of surprise, control, even partnership; and the fecundity of development, as one tin can gave birth to other, only slightly different versions. That development can be seen most obviously in the passage from the Mascot to Republic robot types, as well as in their inspiration for other "tame" robots of the era, perhaps most notably the famous Elektro the Motoman, the aluminum robot star of the Westinghouse Electric pavilion at the 1939–40 New York World's Fair. That figure with rather similar sheet-metal design features, when put through his paces for fair attendees by his human controller, was intended to herald the wonders of electrical living, soon to be realized in what the fair termed "The World of Tomorrow." But they—and he—were just that: wonders that would, disappointingly, have to be put on hold until "tomorrow," or at least for the duration of World War II.

Of course, like other ecologies or complex systems, that of the cinematic robot, of the image that in many ways reflects the constantly changing mechanism of the cinema itself with its mechanical—and now digital—reproduction of lifelike figures, would prove to be an open, not a closed, system. And in that very openness it would make possible other developments, such as those that we shall trace out in the following chapters. Although invariably linked to the Empire's once-new robots, these subsequent figures would emerge in a world where technology hardly surprises us anymore, where it seldom wears a human face (much less a top hat), and where we seem inevitably—for better or worse, as we say—wedded to it, even as we become increasingly wary of its dangers and of our ability to control it.

Notes

1 The Autry National Center, a museum dedicated to Gene Autry and the American West, purchased this piece, which was dated 1933, that is, the year of *Dancing Lady*. For this background I am indebted to Jeffrey Richardson, the Gamble Curator of Western History, Popular Culture, and Firearms of the Autry National Center. For further commentary, see his essay "Cowboys and Robots."

2 See Howard P. Segal's extensive discussion of technology's utopian promise, as well as its failings, in his *Future Imperfect*, especially pp. 164–65.

3 Of course, these images could, in the best tradition of Kuleshovian montage, be read in an opposite way, as suggesting a marriage between woman and machine-man, followed by the woman's disrobing after the wedding, only to then discover that the machine-man she thought she was marrying was, in fact, all machine—and thus, quite the marital disappointment. And with an additional shuffling of these images we might read their implicit narrative differently still, but because we cannot be sure of the intended sequence, our primary concern here is with the implications of each image, all of which, I have suggested, have become part of a robotic ecology of this period.

4 For example, neither Bob Thomas' fan-oriented *Joan Crawford* nor Lawrence Quirk and William Schoell's detailed academic treatment *Joan Crawford: The*

Essential Biography speak to the Machine Age plot elements or remark on the elided scenes described here.

5 Adkins offered this assessment, supported by various production and test stills from Adrian's films, in an e-mail to the author of August 18, 2014.

6 At the same time, the persistence of these images suggests another dimension of the ecology on which we are focused, reminding us how important such pictures were thought to be for helping to sell a film across various media to prospective audiences in Hollywood's pre–Production Code era and how that selling might function appealingly across different types of texts: the film, press releases, advertisements, etc.

7 And "laborer" is precisely what was originally implied by the word "robot," which entered the English language as a result of the Czech play *R. U. R.* (1920) by Karel Capek. In the original Czech the word "robota" translates as compulsory laborer or serf, suggesting both the underclass status of this figure and its primary function as a worker or servant.

8 The "uncanny" seems a fitting description of the way these figures are initially presented and perceived, for as Tzvetan Todorov explains the term, the "uncanny" denotes the "inexplicable," the unusual, or the new that is ultimately judged in terms of "known facts," that is, explained by science, by a changed perspective on the object, or even by reference to past experience (42).

9 One of the most popular of early television series, *Captain Video and His Video Rangers* was also well known for its minimalist aesthetic and slight budgets. It reportedly produced its various visions of an advanced technological world on a special effects budget of just $25 per week. See Fulton, p. 91.

10 The many new, largely electronic devices—often described with pointedly contemporary terms like "atomic," "radar," and "video"—that Captain Video deployed were consistent with what Richard Schwartz describes as an "evolving Cold War belief that scientific and technological superiority would determine the fate of the world" (52).

11 Although the notion of "camp" as an aesthetic category originates in the early twentieth century, it found popular usage in the 1950s and early 1960s. Susan Sontag's famous "Notes on 'Camp'" essay, first published in 1964, traces out the emergence and importance of this concept, particularly in the decade leading up to her remarks.

12 These laws clearly speak to an anxiety that Asimov and others early on sensed in the face of the artificial being, one particularly focused on the issue of control, as repeatedly noted here. Those laws are noted in the introduction.

3   Robby the Robot and Our Electronic Wonders

Advertisements for the film *Forbidden Planet* (1956) almost invariably misrepresented its narrative. Posters, lobby cards, and newspaper ads showed its newly conceived version of the movie robot, Robby, holding the seemingly unconscious and scantily clad girl Altaira (Anne Francis) in its powerful arms, with its domed head and speech box modeled in such a way that they suggested a malevolent scowl and decidedly bad intentions. Primed by a flood of alien invasion and atomic mutation films, audiences of 1956 could not help but anticipate another violent sf adventure, in this case perhaps a story about a robot run amok, even perversely "desiring" a human mate in some atomic-age variation on *Frankenstein*'s image of the monster, similarly carrying off Dr. Frankenstein's new wife in the 1931

Figure 3.1 Robby the Robot as menace in poster for *Forbidden Planet* (1956). MGM.

film, or a more recent variant on this scene, as the Gill Man of *Creature from the Black Lagoon* (1954) in like fashion bore an unconscious Kay Lawrence (Julia Adams) back to his underwater cave. Of course, despite the titillating images, no violations actually occur in any of these films, and in *Forbidden Planet* Robby the Robot proves no more harmful. He essentially functions as Altaira's servant and protector, fully controlled by humans, thanks to that film's introduction of Isaac Asimov's famous Laws of Robotics: those rules expressly designed to contain the implicit dangers of the robotic body sutured to an electronic brain by ensuring that such manifestly powerful figures could not hurt, only efficiently and without question serve their human creators.

However, the misrepresentation offered by the film's advertising is worth considering, not just as one more in a long line of popular images emphasizing women's vulnerability to both primitive and highly techno-logical forces—from which they would, as American films of the 1950s repeatedly suggested, have to be protected by male power—but also as a sign of how the robotic meme was changing valence. Although robots were fairly common in the early Cold War era's sf films, ranging from a work like *The Day the Earth Stood Still* in 1951 to *The Colossus of New York* in 1958, these were not the relatively docile creations of the Machine Age, the tin can figures chronicled in the previous chapter. As that image of Robby suggests, these were figures with, quite literally, minds of their own. These were electronic wonders whose power was lodged not simply in their cold metal chassis, but also in their surprising artificial brains, in this instance emphasized by Robby's glass dome of a head with its circuits and whirring parts all clearly visible. The result is a robot meme that had become terribly conflicted, bound up with both what we hoped technology would do for us and what, in the new age of atomic weaponry, missiles, and computers, we were beginning to suspect it might also do to us.

The nature of that conflicted image becomes especially evident when we consider *Forbidden Planet*'s featured robot from a memetic perspec-tive, that is, as a central component in a larger robot ecology. In this chapter I want to focus on the persistence, consistency, and generation of images that have constellated particularly around *Forbidden Planet*'s influential robot figure—one that, like its tin can predecessors, seemed to set a dominant template for our sense of the robot for several decades, not only in film but also in another new and powerful technological venue, television. A brief history of this most *persistent* figure in all of its vari-ations can help us to better observe and understand the shifting attitudes not just toward such figures, but to a specific formation of mechanical and computer technology that was emerging in the late postwar and early Cold

War era, during the time when Robby lingered, like an archetype of the technological being in the cultural consciousness, a dominant meme in our cultural biology.

Although, as we have seen, Robby the Robot is hardly the first cinematic robot, or even one that bears much resemblance to most of his sf forebears that have previously been described, he is certainly one of the most influential of such film figures, especially when considered in terms of identity, impact, and persistence. For Robby would not only prove a surprise star of *Forbidden Planet*—as his *naming* might well suggest—but, as a result of his popularity (and, in another ecological sense, the simple availability of the very expensive Robby "costume," which also assured a certain visual consistency), he would resurface in another MGM sf effort the following year, *The Invisible Boy* (1957), and he would be featured in a variety of other films into the present time, including *Hollywood Boulevard* (1976), *Gremlins* (1984), *Cherry 2000* (1987), *Earth Girls Are Easy* (1989), and, most recently, *Tomorrowland* (2015). This new electronic wonder, as I have dubbed him and his ilk, would also prove especially popular in another new electronic technology, making "guest" appearances on a great many television shows, among them episodes of *MGM Parade* (1956), *The Perry Como Show* (1956), *The Thin Man* (1958), *The Gale Storm Show* (1958), *The Twilight Zone* (1959, 1963, 1964), *The Many Loves of Dobie Gillis* (1963), *Lost in Space* (1966, 1967), *The Addams Family* (1966, 1967), *The Man from U.N.C.L.E.* (1966), *Columbo* (1974), *Ark II* (1976), *Project UFO* (1978), *Mork and Mindy* (1979), *Wonder Woman* (1979), and *Space Academy* (1979). As a result of these many "star" turns, one commentator would describe him as "the hardest working robot in Hollywood" (Nems). Moreover, Robby would have a long afterlife outside of film and television—as a toy, museum piece, and general component of popular culture.[1] This level of persistence suggests that the Robby "type" touched a cultural sensibility for multiple decades, while establishing in the popular imaginary a new sense of what the robot or artificial being was coming to mean for postwar, atomic-age audiences—as well as for a later generation simply nostalgic for that seemingly more innocent period.

But, as we began by noting, Robby's presentation was conflicted from the start. Print advertising presented him largely as a figure of menace, an icon immediately hinting at the "Forbidden" aspect of the "Planet" Altair IV on which he is first encountered. And the pose with Robby bearing the mainly bare body of Altaira—a scene repeated in most of the advertising for the film—projected a sexual menace, as if, as James Chapman and Nicholas J. Cull have nicely described it, "he had sex on his positronic circuits" (88).[2] Prior to the film's release, Robby was featured in a national publicity campaign offering free tickets to *Forbidden Planet* in boxes of Quaker

Oats. Yet even the ad for that promotion, inserted in children's magazines and comics of the period, depicted not a friendly encounter, but an armed confrontation between three Earthmen and Robby, who seems to tower menacingly over them. Of course, such presentations allowed audiences to anticipate exciting action and adventure, especially by evoking similar robotic images—and actions—with which they might already have been familiar, figures prominently featured in such films as *The Day the Earth Stood Still* (1951), *Gog* (1954), *Tobor the Great* (1954), or even the tellingly titled *Robot Monster* (1953).[3]

And yet even as MGM pushed the dangerous adventure aspect of this, its first sf film of the period, it was also featuring Robby in various promotional appearances on national television—appearances that cast him in a very different light. On the *Today* show, for example, he exchanged light banter with host Dave Garroway, and on *The Perry Como Show* (February 18, 1956), a comedy/variety program, he appears with the film's star Anne Francis in two comic skits, one in which he introduces himself as "president of the Robots for Como fan club" and another in which he plays a cowboy, with a cowboy hat perched precariously atop his glass-domed head. He appears on two episodes of *MGM Parade* (both 1956) where he is interviewed by "co-star" Walter Pidgeon (who plays Morbius, his creator, in *Forbidden Planet*). In the first episode, Pidgeon describes Robby as "a housewife's dream" in light of his described skills at domestic chores, and extant costume tests and publicity stills underscore this side of Robby, as they show him helping Altaira with her shoes and holding her fabric mantle, much like a personal butler. Meanwhile, the Quaker Oats promotion noted earlier was part of a family-directed campaign that paired Robby and *Forbidden Planet* with another MGM release of the same year, the Lucille Ball–Desi Arnaz slapstick comedy *Forever, Darling*, promising free tickets to children attending either film when accompanied by an adult. Robby, it seemed, promised to entertain audiences in a variety of roles, both as imposing antagonist and as comic servant or children's friend. He would, quite simply, become an iconic player in a suddenly popular genre that Susan Sontag would famously define as driven by "the imagination of disaster" (216), while he would also be established as a figure that Vivian Sobchack later described as one of "comic rotundity and comic primness" (8).

Of course, such a dual potential was hardly new to cinematic depictions of the robot. As we have seen, in the 1930s and early 1940s the various tin can or sheet-metal robots, especially those that populated our movie serials, functioned somewhat similarly, both as potential boons to the human realm because of their great power and as possible menaces due to the unpredictable application of that power. Although the Metalogen Man of *The Monster and the Ape* (1945) is designed to "free humans" from heavy labor, he is commandeered by a mad scientist and used for criminal purposes. We might recall *Undersea Kingdom*'s pronouncement that once we learn the "secret" to controlling robots, "all mankind will be relieved of the drudgery of physical labor." However, "control," even in this earlier period, was already becoming a central concern in our relationship to such mechanical technology. Thus, both *Mysterious Doctor Satan* (1940) and *The Monster and the Ape* conclude with their robots going *out of control* and turning, in deadly fashion, on the scientists who created them and sought to use them for evil purposes. And a host of cartoons, such as Farmer Al Falfa's *The Iron Man* (1930), Scrappy's *Technoracket* (1933), Oswald the Lucky Rabbit's *The Mechanical Man* (1932), Flip the Frog's *Techno-Cracked* (1933), and the Superman short *The Mechanical Monsters* (1941), would similarly find robots suddenly going out of control, threatening man, rabbit, and frog alike. But as the introduction noted, this same period saw the publication of a number of more measured robot stories in the pulp magazines, including Isaac Asimov's first efforts wherein he described a complex and, as his tales argue, an inevitably evolving life for robots, while also articulating his famous Laws of Robotics with their explicit purpose of showing how we might control the "positronic" brains of these constructed and potentially dangerous figures, thereby preventing them from harming humans—or developing their own designs on characters like Altaira.

But it is precisely this dimension of Robby the Robot on which we need to focus this memetic investigation, for it is one of the keys to his general consistency in form, his persistence for several decades, and his influence on the development of other related robot images, including some outside of American film (such as John, the very similar robot of the Soviet *Planeta Bur* (*Planet of Storms*, 1962). Although Robby obviously has some physical

Figure 3.2 Robby the Robot introduces himself in *Forbidden Planet* (1956). MGM.

links to those tin-can types that dominated sf cinema for nearly two decades, he also was very different in one key regard. As a print advertisement touted, he is "the most amazing mechanical genius ever devised." And that emphasis on his "genius" was underscored in Bosley Crowther's review of the film, wherein he described Robby as "a phenomenal mechanical man who can do more things in his small body than a roomful of business machines" (Crowther). That allusion to "business machines" was particularly resonant for the time, because 1956 also saw the announcement from IBM that its 704 computer, the latest version of its groundbreaking 700 series, had been programmed not only to play checkers, but to learn from its experiences playing the game, to modify its responses, and thus to demonstrate a primitive form of artificial intelligence. And that development had followed by only a few years the publication of Alan Turing's famous paper "Computing Machinery and Intelligence," with its questioning of how we might draw the line between human and machine intelligence (Kurzweil 69). Moreover, this notion of an artificial intelligence or "mechanical genius"—no matter how limited—along with all that it implied, must have been freighted with as much anxiety as anticipation, because, as Ray Kurzweil describes, it unlocked the door to "a new form of intelligence . . . on Earth," one potentially set in competition with human intelligence (68).

In the process, this emergence of a synthetic intelligence also opened up for exploration a more complex vein of sf cinema: a new regime of robotic types and images. For equipped with such an intelligence, the robot would not only embody the great physical potential of our technology, as we see when Robby carries ten tons of lead shielding in *Forbidden Planet*, but also demonstrate that new potential for competing with the human, as the robot became an autonomous figure driven by an electronic brain—and thus potentially subject to its *own* reasoning and control. Robby's signature glass-domed head, through which we could see relays working and electricity coursing along the pathways of his positronic brain—a feature replicated in *Planeta Bur*'s robot—only emphasized this most distinctive characteristic of the new robotic regime.

This new cinematic figure, designed and created for approximately $100,000 by Arnold Gillespie of MGM's prop department and engineer Robert Kinoshita of the studio's art department, was one of the first "effects" created for the film,[4] in part because, as Frederick S. Clarke and Steve Rubin chronicle, he was conceived to be not just "the most complex of the mechanical props required" for *Forbidden Planet*, but also because he was "to be used extensively throughout the picture," constantly interacting with the main—or human—actors (20). That narrative centrality of the robot, his position as another, and key, player is particularly significant because it positions Robby in a relatively novel position for sf films, as part of the narrative's larger *human* drama, underscoring its central story about the misuse of the mind—and what happens when we are unable to control *its* workings. As the film details, the ancient civilization of the Krel, a "mighty and noble race of beings," formerly inhabited Altair IV. However, they self-destructed after creating machines that provided their minds with the power of "pure instrumentality," that is, with an ability to give shape to matter and use it to accomplish any task they wished. With that liberation of the mind from all physical limitations, there had also come, the film suggests, the liberation of some version of the Freudian id, of the destructive, even murderous, impulses that were otherwise kept in check by the mind's own constraining forces or, in human terms, by the full structure of a truly human personality.

That same loss of control also afflicts Dr. Morbius, the lone survivor of the *Bellerophon* mission that had, many years earlier, been sent to explore and colonize Altair IV. After expanding his mental capacity by using the Krel's mind-training device, he, too, found "freedom" from "physical instrumentality"—but a freedom at a cost similar to that paid by the Krel. For Morbius' new capacities allowed his unconscious to produce an "id monster" that had destroyed all those from the *Bellerophon* party with whom he had disagreed—particularly those who wanted to return to Earth rather than stay on what seemed a most inhospitable planet. Moreover, that monstrous projection was again manifesting itself, beginning to murder crew members of the C57D rescue ship, which he saw as threatening the seemingly idyllic life he had managed to create for himself—a life of the mind spent studying the lost culture of the Krel. When he finally recognizes what has happened—and that he has no way of controlling this monster, given shape and propelled by the nearly limitless forces of the Krel power plants— Morbius, too, succumbs, dying in a confrontation with what he terms his own "evil self," while instructing Commander Adams of the rescue party to throw a switch that will unleash another sort of destructive chain reaction, this one of the Krel furnaces, ensuring the planet's self-destruction, but in the process also reasserting a kind of moral control over the unleashed mind.

It is this linkage of intelligence and control—along with a perceived personality—that would effectively make Robby such a fecund and long-lived model for a new vision of the robot—one that more nearly corresponded to our growing cultural concerns about controlling an increasingly powerful technology. This revised technological meme, as some might term it, is indeed possessed of a complex electronic brain. In fact, Walter Pidgeon emphasizes precisely this feature of the robot in one of the episodes of *MGM Parade* cited earlier wherein Robby was first introduced to a national audience. After "interviewing" the robot in his identity as Morbius, Pidgeon pauses and wonders if Robby does "really have a brain?" That query is followed by a long shot of Robby standing alone in a dark corner of the studio, his lights and circuits working away, while we hear a demonic laugh emanating from his neon-lit voice box.

But that troubling notion is consistent with his ambiguous presentation in the film. Tinkered together by Morbius with the aid of the Krel's advanced technology, Robby embodies that culture's advanced thinking—thinking that also, as we have noted, led to its destruction. Consistently, we see him taking in data through various sensory apparati, drawing conclusions, and recommending responses, as when he senses the approach of the invisible "monster from the id," as it is described, warns the humans at Dr. Morbius' compound, activates defenses against it, yet also does not shoot it with his defensive ray precisely because he understands—as the humans do not—that it is a part of Morbius' own psyche and to attack it would mean attacking his master. If that failure to respond defensively at first seems disconcerting, as if he were either complicit or irresponsible in the events on Altair IV, it eventually becomes a point of reassurance, because his reluctance to act is the surest sign of Robby's control by the film's version of Asimov's rules, here described by Morbius as the robot's "basic inhibition to harm rational beings," coupled with an "absolute selfless obedience" to humans. So although Robby is initially suspected of being the very monster that is murdering the crew of the C57D—the menace so strongly suggested in much of the film's advertising—his protocols guarantee that, despite his prodigious powers and an apparent mind of his own, he will remain safely subservient to, even *concerned* for, his human companions. And as a final demonstration of both those controls and the humans' faith in them, the film concludes with Robby being inducted into the crew of the C57D as a replacement for the ship's murdered navigator. That position affirms that the humans' ability to return home (both physically and psychologically), to locate a world where we still have, as Commander Adams observes, "laws and religions" to help us control the various "monsters in our subconscious," is safely lodged in the robot's capable and fully controlled claws.

Perhaps it is this sense of safety or control that would allow for another adaptation of that form, while also demonstrating an element of "fecundity" in its use, as Robby, in the wake of *Forbidden Planet*'s wide success, was quickly pirated as a children's tin toy. Although the toy robot easily predates Robby's screen appearance,[5] toy collector and historian Teruhisa Kitahara observes that probably "the favorite toy of the fifties was the robot," a figure that often "inspired a strange mixture of fear and anticipation" (110). In fact, the tin metal robot would become a centerpiece of the Japanese toy industry in the 1950s, with, as Ron Tanner reports in his study of this industry, toy robots accounting "for as much as one-sixth of the catalog of toy exports" from Japan to the United States. And although these toy designs generally "changed yearly or every other year" (80), Robby in particular became one of the most popular and longest-lived templates for this conflicted figure.

Thus, throughout the late 1950s and well into the 1960s Japan exported a wide variety of toys in Robby's image, sporting, as Kitahara notes, an appealing combination of "tin plate, flashing lights, and rasping gears" (110). Among this group, the Nomura Toy Company would produce both a walking, battery-powered version—which, with little regard to copyright issues, they forthrightly dubbed "Robby"—and a wired, multifunction, remote-controlled version. The Yoshiya Company would manufacture a less complex, wind-up version in multiple colors that it more generically dubbed "Robot Space Trooper." Yonizawa created a spring-driven "Mechanical Moon Robot" version of Robby that was a bit more menacing, thanks to its ability to spit sparks from its mouthpiece. And Yoshiya would even provide an alternative identity for its Robby by also issuing it with a human face depicted inside of its glass-domed head and labeling it "Moon Explorer," thus underscoring the partnership between the robot's prodigious physical form and a guiding *human* intelligence that seemingly inhabited it. These and other versions not only point up the wide appeal and persistence of the Robby image in the cultural imaginary—both in the United States and elsewhere—but they also suggest a significant element of that appeal: how children might play out that narrative of control bound up in this figure, powering up and remotely controlling their own Robby, perhaps even—in the example of the "Moon Explorer" version—imaginatively inhabiting his powerful form, thereby properly linking his prodigious mechanical force with a human brain.

That sense of the robot as a rather sophisticated technological toy would also persist and provide a part of the context for MGM's spin-off from

Figure 3.3 Mechanized Robot—Robby the Robot toys from the 1950s.

Forbidden Planet, The Invisible Boy, although that film would focus even more directly on our anxieties about the proper linkage between technology and the brain that increasingly haunted 1950s culture. Capitalizing on Robby's popularity—while helping to amortize that expensive robot costume—*The Invisible Boy* was a low-budget effort that reunited *Forbidden Planet*'s producer Nicholas Nayfack with its key writers, Cyril Hume and Irving Block, in a narrative adapted from a *Saturday Evening Post* short story "The Story of Timothy—The World's Worst Problem Child." Although Robby would figure centrally in the film, it is telling that the source story contained no robot, focusing instead on a young boy who chronically misbehaves. But in an effort to recall elements of the original film and establish its identity as a sequel of sorts, *The Invisible Boy* would portray its child protagonist not as a "problem," after the fashion of the many wayward youth films of the 1950s, but rather as a bored yet curious boy whose mind is invaded and, like Morbius, enhanced by a supercomputer that his father, Professor Merinoe, has developed at the Stoneman Institute of Mathematics. Transformed into a genius by the computer, young Timmy is prodded to ask his father if he can play with a junked robot—Robby—which, with the computer's secret aid, he surprisingly manages to put together and turn into an amazing and dangerous toy/playmate.

Advertised in similar fashion to *Forbidden Planet, The Invisible Boy*'s posters show Robby prominently posed, holding the boy in his claws, as various tanks, guns, and missiles seemingly fire towards him, while a headline proclaims: "The science-monster who would destroy the world!" But here, too, the publicity materials from the start painted Robby wrongly, as a potential menace, no longer kept in check by Asimovian controls on his robotic brain. He is, as we learn, a powerful tool that the computer wants to use in its own efforts to take over the world. Thus, the real struggle that emerges in this film is not so much with Robby, with an artificial being gone out of control, as it is with Merinoe's supercomputer, that disembodied brain, containing, as its inventor proudly explains, "the sum total of human knowledge." However, what Robby helps foreground is a significant blindness afflicting that "total . . . knowledge," that is, our human inability to understand the dangerous potential of the vast store of knowledge that the scientists were, in effect, liberating. Robby, we learn, had been brought back from the future—apparently from the time in which *Forbidden Planet*'s narrative takes place—as a result of an experiment with time travel, but this fantastic piece of technology had since fallen into neglect and disrepair because the institute's scientists had become obsessed with something even more alluring—the possibility of creating a "supermind" or supercomputer. When resurrected by Timmy, Robby demonstrates that he has been programmed with "basic directives," precisely the sort of controls that would prevent him from doing things that might harm young Timmy—or any other humans. However, the computer quickly reprograms him and, in the process, establishes itself as his "master," just as it then begins doing with the various scientists and military officials who work at the institute. Self-aware, armed with massive knowledge, and powered by its own nuclear reactor, the electronic brain eventually reveals itself as the real "science-monster" promised by the film's advertising, as it introduces changes into its "feedback system," giving it unimpeded thought, as well as its own id-like desires, and it sets about using Robby and the various scientists of the institute to hijack a military satellite that it plans to use in its plot to take over the Earth.

In keeping with its development of Robby as a kind of large toy, *The Invisible Boy*'s answer to that threat of the electronic brain is a simple but also finally a reassuring one. Concerned for young Timmy's safety—as the computer threatens the boy in order to coerce his father's cooperation—Robby manifests an ability to resist his new "master," to resist being transformed from a toy into a terror weapon, and reverts to his "original basic directives." And although the computer still manages to stop Professor Merinoe from destroying it, first by hypnotizing him with its flashing lights and then by offering him a familiar Faustian bargain—a promise of unlimited knowledge and power, "if only you will serve and obey me," as it says—Robby's directives prove more resolute than any frail human will-power. Recognizing the larger threat to humanity, Robby effectively saves mankind from itself by destroying the computer's circuits and stopping the full "revolt of the machines" that, we are told, these events portend. In its own, almost playful way, *The Invisible Boy* thus sounds a warning against that marriage of an advanced electronic brain with the physical power of a robot unconstrained by Asimovian rules. In splitting off the computer brain from the robot's fantastic body in this way, in temporarily enslaving Robby to a machine with more thought power than either himself or any humans, the film points to a troubling anxiety that had become attached to our conceptions of the robot, and indeed to much technology: a fear not so much of its physical power, as had been the case in its earlier incarnations, but of its *thought* power—and of the dangerous step that combining powerful thinking and doing machines might constitute.

It is an anxiety that would not only continue in our culture, but that would be reflected in the very longevity that Robby would demonstrate. As mentioned earlier, he would continue to be featured in a long list of films and television shows. And in keeping with the patterns noted earlier, some of those appearances would be largely comic in nature, whereas others were more consistent with those dangerous or disturbing possibilities observed in *The Invisible Boy*. Robby would, for example, surface prominently in multiple episodes of *The Twilight Zone*, easily the key television venue of the late 1950s and early 1960s for sf. As Rodney Hill offers, the series addressed a variety of closely related cultural "fears" bound up in the sf imagination: "of technological and cultural change, of the future, of the unknown" (115). Of course, as we think ecologically, we should hardly be surprised by Robby's appearances on *The Twilight Zone*, because most episodes of that series were shot on the MGM lot with full access to the studio's vast store of props. In fact, a number of other props and costumes from *Forbidden Planet* would, from time to time, appear on the show, as when one of the most famous episodes, "The Monsters Are Due on Maple Street" (March 4, 1960), used the film's spaceship, spacesuits, and other props to depict alien invaders. Such uses were simply evidence of what we might see as a big studio's own complex ecological system.

More interestingly, though, Robby would function variously across the spectrum of meanings we have already described, suggesting that all were simultaneously in play. For example, in the first of these appearances, "One for the Angels" (October 9, 1959), he is indeed a small wind-up toy of the sort that Kitahara frequently catalogs, one of many that we see sidewalk pitchman Lou Bookman selling to kids on the street—along with various other spaceman toys, ties, collar stays, and sundry goods. Because these figures would have had to be fashioned or purchased expressly for this episode, his appearance here seems, on the one hand, to be partly an homage to the fidelity and longevity of the Robby image, a testimony to the way that this version of the robot—in spite of the many others that had appeared throughout the 1950s—had powerfully imprinted itself on our cultural imaginations. Yet on the other, to those familiar with the image, it also seems an initial clue to the episode's uncanny thrust, an early warning about the "twilight zone" into which Bookman is about to enter as he is drawn into making a deal with Death to save a youngster's life.

Operating more in the vein of *The Invisible Boy* is the serio-comic episode "The Brain Center at Whipple's" (May 15, 1964), a narrative about automation and the inevitable replacement of humans by machines. As in that film, the show centers on a massive computer, the new "brain center" that factory owner Wallace Whipple has installed to help run his company more efficiently. As he explains to one of his recently fired employees, the new computer represents "progress," because it will eliminate 61,000 jobs and seventy-three machines, do away with time clocks, and save the company approximately $4,000,000 per year. That litany did, of course, echo with both factual and feared results from a rising tide of computer-driven automation in American industry during this period, as well as the widespread adoption of the IBM 700-series machines that had demonstrated a primitive possibility for artificial intelligence. But the show would also use Robby to move beyond simply corroborating the outcome of what narrator Rod Serling terms "the historic struggle between the brain of man and the product of man's brain." For in a comic version of *The Twilight Zone*'s familiar twist endings, the computer's success ironically results in Whipple, too, becoming outmoded, as we see when Whipple is fired and Robby walks into his office, twirls his office keys, and answers his phone. Guided by a super-efficient brain, the machine, it seems, has determined that man, even at the highest levels, is just a figure of "obsolescence," and thanks to our unwitting cooperation it stands ready to replace us all.

Building even more darkly on this sort of replacement strategy, the episode "Uncle Simon" (November 15, 1963) describes how an aged inventor produces a robot—once again Robby but with a partial and rather unpleasant face inserted within his glass-domed head—into the electronic brain of which he downloads his own personality. However, his purpose is not simply to replace himself or gain a longer, artificial life, but rather to take lasting vengeance upon his grubbing and embittered niece who has reluctantly served him in hopes of eventually acquiring his fortune. Discovered after Uncle Simon's death, the robot gradually takes on various characteristics of the uncle, but especially his constant verbal and mental abuse of the girl, while she gains his fortune but is reduced, by the terms of her uncle's will, to nothing more than the machine's slave—ironically, the *worker* that robots were once supposed to replace, as well as an abject warning against abdicating or subordinating the self to the machine or the promise of wealth. Programmed with and driven by man's worst impulses, the brain buttressed

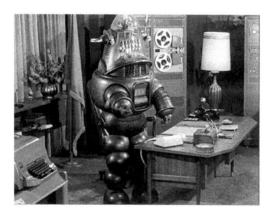

Figure 3.4 Robby the Robot as emblem of automation in *The Twilight Zone*'s "The Brain Center at Whipple's" (1964). MGM.

by a robotic body here offers no payback, only the promise to make human servitude a permanent thing, reversing the supposed roles of the worker and its creator/master.

And yet Robby did not linger in the cultural imaginary simply because he foregrounded these sorts of negative or dangerous possibilities that the combination of robotic body and electronic brain increasingly seemed to forecast. As Irving Block, one of *Forbidden Planet*'s writers, observed, despite the sort of conflicted media images and plot lines—or even MGM's own publicity materials—that at times seemed to paint him as "a heavy," Robby had originally been "conceived as a good robot, not a destructive machine" (Clarke and Rubin 65). Functioning within that original conception, he continued to serve, especially in episodes of popular comedy series, such as *The Many Loves of Dobie Gillis*, *The Addams Family*, and *Mork and Mindy*, largely because he managed through the 1960s and into the 1970s to hold the physical presence of the robot in some harmony with the new and potentially disturbing potential of electronic intelligence that he also embodied. It is, actually, a rather tense relationship that we can perhaps best view at work in another of these series, *Lost in Space*, a show that not only used Robby as a "guest star" on several occasions, but also offered perhaps the best example of that image's fecundity with its own version of the Robby template, Robot B-9, or the General Utility Non-Theorizing Environmental Control Robot—usually simply addressed as "Robot" and often, because of a general physical similarity, in subsequent historical accounts of the series confused with Robby.

When producer Irwin Allen first began work on his new adventure–comedy series *Lost in Space*, he fittingly hired the well-versed Robert Kinoshita to design a new robot (or, more precisely, robot costume) that might be appropriate for a family-oriented show. Drawing on his previous experience at MGM, as well as the multiple possibilities that had clustered around his prior creation, Kinoshita made Robot very much in the image of the persistent Robby, with a glass-domed yet differently shaped head, bulbous body, and similarly stocky appendages. Thanks to the use of more flexible materials, Robot's look was decidedly softened from that of his predecessor, and particularly in those instances when it would wildly wave his hose-like arms in a sort of robotic panic, warning of some approaching danger or emergency, it seemed well suited to the mixed tone of Allen's show. Yet Robot is more than simply a semifamiliar and indeed iconic connection to *Forbidden Planet* and to the various appearances of Robby and near-Robbies over several decades. He helps to foreground both the best hopes and worst fears that, over the period, had become attached to this sort of mind-ful figure.

Conceived as a primary resource for the Robinson family expedition, a technological "man Friday" for these futuristic Crusoes who, as in the case of *Forbidden Planet*'s *Bellerophon* mission, have been sent on a deep-space colonization mission, Robot is originally sabotaged and commandeered by stowaway Dr. Zachary Smith. Early in the series, Smith several times uses Robot to menace the Robinsons, and at one point he even disconcertingly—and dispassionately, as if he were himself more robotic than human—instructs it to do away with all "nonessential personnel." Yet Robot is eventually reprogrammed, and as the series made a turn from straight action-adventure to a more comic mode, he would become a personal companion to and protector of the Robinsons' young son, Will, as well as a constant foil for Dr. Smith's increasingly comic-toned and usually inept villainy. Although strong, in the tradition of Robby and earlier robots, armed with defensive weapons, and possessed of advanced intelligence and a storehouse of important information, Robot is more than simply a supreme technological tool—a futuristic Swiss army knife with a brain. Rather, in the course of the series he develops a decidedly human persona. In fact, actor Bob May, who portrayed the mechanical figure, notes that producer Irwin Allen encouraged him to develop Robot in more or less human ways; as he explains, the "plan . . . was to give it that ultimate personality so that the other actors would not look at it as" simply a machine (May). Thus we see Robot playing baseball with Will, fishing, even strumming a guitar, as he becomes an essential part of this lost *human* expedition. And by the series' final episode "Junkyard in Space" (March 6, 1968), Robot actually makes a very human sacrifice, agreeing to trade parts of himself, including his precious memory banks, to a decidedly uncomic robotic junkman who has imprisoned the Robinson family. The result is a highly emotional farewell between Will and his mechanical best friend, who is prepared to give his "life" for those of his companions.

That humanization of Robot, though, occurs in parallel with—and in stark contrast to—the series' introduction of various other, less "friendly" mechanical types, such as that robotic junkman of "Junkyard in Space." Robot seems to suggest that by reinforcing those fundamental Asimovian rules with placement in an appropriate human realm—a realm that can allow his artificial intelligence to learn about people and thus make him more like them—the mechanical being might become a valued member of society and an important extension of what it means to be alive. But at the same time, other robots continue to remind us of the mechanical being's parallel and more dangerous potential. In fact, Robot would even be set in opposition with his template, Robby, in several episodes, with Robby each time ironically embodying that darker side of our electronic wonders. For example, in the episode "Condemned of Space" (September 6, 1967), the Robinson expedition must rescue Robot when he is accidentally trapped in a space prison, one where Robby also appears, portraying an unsympathetic jailer

Figure 3.5 Robot B-9 with Will Robinson (Billy Mumy) in *Lost in Space* (1965–68). CBS.

who, like a machine with only limited capacities, refuses to budge from his primary directive, which is to keep everyone on the planet imprisoned, including the Robinsons who have come only as rescuers. In another, "War of the Robots" (February 9, 1966), Robby appears as Robotoid, a machine with a far more complex, even devious, capacity. It slyly ingratiates itself among the Robinsons as a more modern and capable replacement for Robot. However, when young Will accidentally learns that Robotoid's benevolence is just a pose and that he serves an alien who is hoping to capture the Robinson expedition, he and Robot—human and machine—combine forces to thwart the alien's plans, in the process demonstrating Robot's unwavering concern for the welfare of his human companions, even though they had appeared ready to reject him for a "better model." In both cases, the problem posed by these robotic pairs set in conflict is one of minds: as a mind that values the human is juxtaposed with ones that do not, that are even duplicitous, and that thus pose a danger to humanity.

That repeated comparison of two quite similar—and persistent—versions of this figure suggests a consistent level of doubt or worry that still attended this popular image of the robot. It is as if the Robby type, for all of its lingering popularity—and indeed, it would continue to surface in various film and television texts for more than a decade, although increasingly as a kind of nostalgic signpost—had managed to mollify our anxieties about such robots, and particularly about their electronic brains, only partially or temporarily. We might note that just a few years after *Lost in Space* left the air, another sort of electronic aid, human caretaker, even a seemingly interested friend to man, the HAL 9000 computer of *2001: A Space Odyssey* (1968), would inexplicably go berserk, killing off most of the astronauts it was supposed to support on their mission to Jupiter. And shortly after, *Westworld* (1973), along with its sequel *Futureworld* (1976), would depict its theme park robots (or audioanimatronics), figures that had been programmed to provide any sort of pleasure park visitors might desire, similarly developing unexpectedly violent tendencies and simply killing off the guests. Despite their human seeming, even a constructed sexual appeal in the *Westworld/Futureworld* figures, something of the uncanny and disturbing spirit of these robots simply refused to be dispelled.

Jane Bennett, in her influential work on what she terms the "ecology of things," has described a similar sort of troubled human response to the natural world today. Following the lead of Bruno Latour, she notes how even as "the modern self feels increasingly *entangled*—cosmically, biotechnologically, medically, virally, pharmacologically—with nonhuman nature," and even as that "commingling has . . . become harder to ignore," there remains a human tendency to pull back, to reassert "the boundary between culture and nature," as well as "machines" (*Vibrant* 115), as if all that is not human can have that same uncanny effect on us. Although the wondrous electronic brains of these robots, either when properly programmed or simply through extended human interaction, would, as we have seen, allow them to serve as playthings, companions, protectors, comic foils, even "friends," there lingered that sense of "boundary," whether because of the robot's very nature or, as Bennett might suggest, because of a human inability to embrace "the intimacy of the human and the nonhuman" (116), to recognize our similarly "living" nature.

As films like *Westworld*, *Futureworld*, and the similar *The Stepford Wives* (1975) already forecast, the robot of the sf cinema would, as Robby's once-dominant image began to wane, increasingly challenge that notion of boundary. Largely abandoning that figure's "comic rotundity" and playful aspect, it would gradually assume a new, more pointedly anthropomorphic form. Although Robby, like his tin-can predecessors, managed an amazing longevity, although the image remained remarkably faithful to its original visual conception, and although it was fecund enough to inspire similar types (not just *Lost in Space*'s Robot, but a host of other brainy figures, including the title character of *The Colossus of New York* [1958], John of *Planeta Bur*, and even the guardian robot of *Logan's Run* [1976]) and to suggest various possibilities for the electronic-brained robot (both good and bad), this figure that had, as the early posters predicted, swept the culture up in its mechanical arms but operated according to its own and disturbingly unpredictable "positronic circuits," would eventually be replaced in our cultural imaginary by various sorts of replicants, cyborgs, and androids—all at least *looking* just like us. But Robby's persistence in our films, television programs, and even toy counters singularly marks an era between the 1950s and 1970s when we sought, with both difficulty and trepidation, to meld the promise of pre-war, Machine Age technology with the new postwar possibilities of the computer, the electronic brain, and artificial intelligence as we culturally subjected the robot to its own sort of Turing Test.

Of course, today the electronic brain—the computer and its various off-spring, including the ubiquitous *smart* phone—lives among us. Without it much of both our work and our play would simply stop—a situation that we would prefer not to contemplate. But the image of Robby and his imitators lingers as part of a larger ecology of the intersection of computing and auto-mation.[6] That Robby could in this earlier period translate into both friend and enemy, seem like a child's innocent toy as well as a rapacious predator, even a replacement for the human, underscores our conflicted sense of how successfully we might be able to negotiate those great possibilities of new technology. And as a parade of finely detailed, fully anthropomorphized, and immensely powerful cyborg successors appearing across a wide range of films, television programs, and video games have repeatedly demon-strated, it is a problem that continues to fascinate our media and to challenge the sf imagination.

Notes

1 For a more extensive listing of Robby's many film and television credits, see Mark Nems' "Robby the Robot Filmography."

2 Of course, this positioning of Robby as a potential *sexual* menace was hardly unique to advertising in this period. Posters and lobby cards for various other films of this period, including *The Day the Earth Stood Still* (1951), *The Colossus of New York* (1959), and *The Atomic Monster* (1958), reiterated this theme, and *Tobor the Great* (1954), featuring a very similar robot, not only showed the mechani-cal figure carrying off a partially clad female, but offered a legend suggestively describing the robot as a "Man-Made Monster with *Every* Human Emotion."

3 For a discussion of this recurrent sf motif in posters, lobby cards, and advertis-ing literature of the 1950s, see my "Sex and Machines: The 'Buzz' of 1950s Science Fiction."

4 It is worth underscoring here that Robby was, finally, just a "costume," a mechanical seeming figure that, as was the case with the tin can robots of an earlier era, had to be inhabited by a human actor. That habitation was, in this instance, particularly meaningful, because Frankie Darro, Gene Autry's "ward" in *The Phantom Empire* who so easily understood and explained the workings of Murania's metal men, took on the role of Robby, thereby linking these two very different interpretations of the robot figure.

5 As Mark Young et al. chronicle, the Archer Company in the United States pro-
duced several sets of "Space Man" toys in plastic, including robot figures (96).
Other tin robots produced in Japan go back to the early postwar period with the
Liliput Robot being produced by the KT Company and Atomic Robot Man by
Alps, both in 1948.

6 Today one can not only purchase a life-sized, "fully functional" version of
Robby, re-created from original plans by Fred Barton, but also see a copy within
a context that attests to Robby's place in this larger "ecology," that is, the Robot
Hall of Fame at Carnegie Mellon University. See Fred Barton's Internet site
www.the-robotman.com.

4   In Our Image
The Robot as "Skin Job"

As early as Fritz Lang's sf epic *Metropolis* (1927), the metallic robot created by the scientist Rotwang would demonstrate one of the ultimate problems associated with this figure. To test the power of his creation, Rotwang gives it a human appearance, making it *look* exactly like Maria, a leader of the city's repressed workers. And to test out the power of this illusion, he has the robotic Maria perform a strip-tease dance before the young men of the city—a performance that, as she removes various veils and coverings, getting down to her simulated skin, quite literally seduces them into a kind of mad frenzy, prompting them to fight and even kill over her, in effect to become something less than human, while also forecasting her similar effect, seen later in the narrative, when she seduces the workers of the city as well, leading them into a riot of self-destruction. To no surprise, it seems that looking like an especially attractive woman, that being cast as a visual spectacle, that skin itself can be quite powerful, although that gender commentary is hardly at the core of Lang's film. Rather, he wants to suggest how easily we are seduced by appearances of all sorts—a beautiful body, majestic skyscrapers, and especially powerful technology with all of its newness and seeming benefits. More precisely, though, it is the disjunction between that attractive-seeming and the potentially damaging reality it disguises that he wants to lay bare, particularly through the vehicle of his film's mesmerizing skin-covered robot and her visual appeal.

"Skin jobs" like Maria, such nearly perfect simulacra of the human, have appeared in our movies nearly from the time of the first films, although as the preceding chapters illustrate, they would not become commonplace, not become persistent sf memes until much later.[1] As the previous chapters have outlined, we would pass through decades of cinematic fascination with very different sorts of robots, covered in a different sort of "skin." Especially clumsily moving metallic figures—the metal projecting its own powerful aura of strength and invulnerability, but also a readily observable *difference* from the human—would hold sway over our imaginations before the notion of the robot would find a new and especially fertile climate in the products of our newly developing biotechnologies, the rising interest in genetic engineering, and a changing sense of what the robot might be, do, or represent. That climate would produce the possibility of androids, cyborgs, and replicants, the last of these explicitly—and disparagingly, with an eye to another sort of surface evaluation, that of racism—referred to as "skin jobs" in one of the landmark sf films about this subject, Ridley Scott's *Blade Runner* (1982). But that fascination with the outer covering, the "skin," as it were, as well as with something that accompanies it, the gaze that these human-seeming figures almost invariably seem to engage, would generate its own ecological pattern, or as we have previously offered, its own display of "fecundity, fidelity, and longevity" that has added an important dimension to sf cinema.

In fact, this robot-that-does-not-look-like-a-robot might arguably be—and perhaps paradoxically, given its *nonrobotic* appearance—the most compelling of those various artificial being images that our sf films, throughout their history and as one of their key generic signatures, have conjured up for our consideration. Its fundamental nature, as technology given a human appearance, and at times a quite human behavior, affords a telling reflection of what sf, at its most basic point, is all about: the human technologized—or rather, the human confronting and accommodating himself or herself to the imperatives of a world of science and technology, a world that promises to remake the human in its own image, in fact, a world that, rather like film itself, forcefully confronts us with its own sort of vitality. But the important

Figure 4.1 The skin job Pris (Daryl Hannah) hides among a welter of toys, dolls, and robots in *Blade Runner* (1982). Warner Bros.

shift marked by the skin job is its concern not so much with the sheer power of a robotic body or even with the intelligence that directs it—the chief interests of those earlier robotic films we have examined—but rather its emphasis on surfaces, on that human seeming. For with that appearance it is especially able to interrogate our own seemliness, that is, how we act as humans, as well as to reflect on the nature of our films, which have always been, on one level, *about appearances.* In sum, this figure's skin-iness is central to its attraction, binding up both the appeal and the anxieties that this sort of robot so compellingly embodies, while framing them in the context of film's own manifest attractions.

In focusing attention on this version of the robotic being and on this sense of its appeal, I am, from the start, essentially collapsing what some would see as an important technical distinction. Although scientists and sf authors alike often emphasize the nuances between three different formulations of artificial beings—of android, cyborg, and replicant[2]—most of our sf films, as well as much of the popular consciousness, usually blur the defining boundaries, with androids, replicants, and cyborgs, whether built, grown, or a combination of the two, all becoming variant names for a new class of robotic beings: figures that look largely like us but that, because of their advanced engineering, most often have mechanical or biological enhancements, and in some cases built-in limitations as well. Yet whether they are physically stronger, more beautiful, more intelligent, have far greater memory *capacity* (but lacking *personal* memories), have shorter or longer lifespans—most of these the case with *Blade Runner*'s replicants— as a group these inheritors of the robot's cinematic mantle invariably seem to suggest a new sort of anxiety bound up in their—and, by implication, *our own*—image, and one not typically attached to earlier formulations of the robot. It is, as I have suggested, an anxiety largely connected to that very likeness, their *similarity* to the human and what it might imply for our future. More than simply a fear that, as films like *The Human Duplicators* (1965) and *The Stepford Wives* (1975) early on envisioned, we might be easily, even unobtrusively, replaced by perfect copies of the self, these simulacra crystalize a problem that, as we have noted, was often linked to previous robotic figures and their creators. Their creation speaks to a desire for an almost god-like status, with their scientist-makers demonstrating a nearly divine ability to create figures *precisely* in our own image, often figured as a transformative ability to turn base objects into vital subjects. However, in most such creation narratives that human seeming proves to be somewhat more than skin deep. In fact, because of that potential depth, because of what lies *below* the skin and cannot be so easily seen, they usually prove even more disturbing than earlier regimes of robots, more a threat to our own status than their simple mechanical brethren, because their being and actions together hold out the possibility of a new measure of the human—as they do things we cannot do or, in our more inhumane moments, things we no longer do—and even a level on which the human, finally, might somehow seem a lesser and perhaps no longer necessary creation. It is on this complex connection between surface or skin and what lies beneath that this chapter will essentially focus.

This sort of vision was central to that foundational text for all subsequent robot stories, Karel Capek's *R. U. R.* (1920), the play that would introduce the word "robot" from the Czech into the English vocabulary. In that play, robotic workers, shaped from a chemically produced protoplasm that allows them to have a fully human appearance, have taken over much of the world's labor. In relatively short order, as every country is seduced by the promise of robotic workers, they become practically essential to the worldwide economy. But because they can think for themselves, reason as well as labor, they begin to make decisions about their place in the world. The robots quickly become discontented with their subservient status, revolt against their human creators and supposed masters, and eventually kill all the humans, save for Alquist, a technician whom they find useful. When robots begin to wear out and no more are being fashioned, they turn to him to rediscover the formula for robotic creation. Although Alquist does not have that nearly divine skill to create in his own image—or theirs—he discovers that, because they have developed emotions, even demonstrated love for each other, because their semblance to humans has actually gone far more than skin deep, they might also have the capacity for procreation, in effect, the ability to form a new human race. And although this human-looking race would be fundamentally different from their creators, in much the way that contemporary humans differ from earlier human forms such as Neanderthals or Cro-Magnons, they would represent a new and perhaps even better form of humanity. Seen in this light, *R. U. R.* is ultimately a hopeful story about technological regeneration, perhaps even a kind of necessary human perfection through technology. However, the play, produced in the full flowering of the Machine Age, also points up the danger inherent in such skin jobs. For these creations not only suggest where our seductive technologies might be heading, but they also become a dark mirror of our fragile human identity in the face of that era's dizzying scientific and technological development, reflecting both our desire for power and, it seems, for powerlessness, even oblivion—an outcome all too easily envisioned in the wake of the highly mechanized destruction that had recently been wrought by World War I.

As noted earlier, this version of the robot appears from time to time throughout film history, but typically with little effort to limn the logic or science behind the development of such beings. The skin job would only begin to dominate depictions of artificial life in the late 1970s and early 1980s as technological circumstances began to suggest not only a scientific possibility, but even a kind of inevitability to their development. An early and quite innocent version of this figure would appear in the theme park audioanimatronics developed for Disneyland, the 1964 New York World's Fair, and Walt Disney World, all heavily publicized on the Disney television series in the 1950s and 1960s, and all enthusiastically received as technological wonders or, quite literally, *attractions*, and thus by no means threatening developments. However, that status would quickly—and rather directly—be interrogated by films like *Westworld* (1973) and *Futureworld* (1976), both about adult theme parks whose central features were such robotic attractions. Although enormously appealing because of the way they allow humans to act out their desires with a compliant, human-seeming underclass, the parks easily turn from *Metropolis*-style pleasure gardens to technological terrors. For in each instance, the park's robots go out of control, acting not just as if there were problems in their programming, but as if they, too, had minds of their own, robotic agendas that lead them to begin killing off the guests. And these cautionary tales about our inability to "trust" robots, especially those that look and act like us, that easily stand in for humans in both work and play, would open the door to a wealth of other skin job films that resurface the issue of control, with *Blade Runner* probably the most influential among them.

Because this study is not a *history* of such films, but rather an ecological discussion, an effort to examine the breadth and relationship of these robotic figures, I want to focus attention on the most persistent formulations of the skin job—works that have most helped to shape this figure's cultural environment. This new robot type, I would argue, finds its most telling— and perhaps its most persistent—manifestation in the various titular figures from the series of *Terminator* texts: the feature films *The Terminator* (1984), *Terminator 2: Judgment Day* (1991), *Terminator 3: Rise of the Machines* (2003), *Terminator Salvation* (2009), and *Terminator Genisys* (2015), as well as the short-lived television series *Terminator: The Sarah Connor Chronicles* (2008–09), and even the Universal Studios theme park attraction *Terminator 2 3-D* (1996), which effectively revisions the plot of *Terminator 2*. These works all explore the same premise that we saw as central to the electronic wonder films, that is, the implications of creating an advanced synthetic brain: one that attains self-consciousness, that expands its reasoning abilities far beyond those of its creators, and that eventually plots the eradication of what it judges to be a lesser sort of creation—humans. When that initial plot goes awry and humans resist the robotic takeover, this brain, the intelligence network Skynet, produces various cyborg "terminators" to help in its fight against the humans and, over the course of the films, television series, and theme park show (which combines a 3-D film with a live-action component), it sends several such figures back in time in hope of stopping the origins of the human struggle against the machine takeover by killing Sarah Connor and/or her son John, the two leading figures of the human resistance. But clearly, it is not just the development of the super-computer, not just our long-standing anxiety about artificial intelligence that is the target of these works, as their very titles should point up—for their emphasis is, as in the case of even an early text such as *R. U. R.*, distinctly on the possible *termination* of the human, a consequence abetted by the ability to fashion robots that seem like perfect human simulacra.

In fact, over the series' course the *Terminator* films propose different variations on their signature terminator character, each one suggesting other dangers—as well as other possibilities—bound up in such simulacra, although most of them linked to our own inability to distinguish them from real humans. The first film, for instance, largely focuses on sketching the nature of that figure, as played by Arnold Schwarzenegger. He is power-ful in the vein of the traditional metal robot, guided by an on-board com-puter that makes tremendous stores of information immediately available to him, and, once he acquires appropriate clothing, easily passes for human. Because he does so easily pass—in spite of the rather exaggerated human form projected by the champion bodybuilder Schwarzenegger—he is able to extract additional information from other humans in his search for the right Sarah Connor in a city that contains multiple characters with the same

Figure 4.2 The skin job as menacing biker (Arnold Schwarzenegger) in *Terminator 2* (1991). Tristar Pictures.

name. In fact, without arousing suspicion, he even manages to walk into a police station where she is supposedly under heavy police "protection." In effect, his closeness in appearance allows him to get close to his intended human victim, while surprising those who might otherwise intervene, and that closeness here heralds what we are told is his singular purpose, to "terminate" Sarah and, with that mission accomplished, humanity as well, because she, as the mother of the resistance leader, is its last hope against a machine hegemony.

Perhaps the terminator's most memorable line in this first film is his promise, uttered at the police station, "I'll be back." It is a promise that forecasts not only the figure's next plot move, as he returns heavily armed, invades the station, and kills all who resist, but also the persistence of this skin job in the cultural imaginary, particularly as he and his successors return in the various film sequels and, in fact, as the line itself becomes a series signature, being repeated with a promise of further returns (that is, additional films and additional *box office* returns) in subsequent franchise entries. The complications introduced in the first sequel, *Terminator 2*, are especially drawn out of this problematic of appearance. A terminator (once more played by Schwarzenegger), looking just like the one from the first film and assuming the dress of a menacing biker, is again sent back in time, but in this instance to help Sarah as well as her now-teenaged son John avoid assassination. Although in a variation on the Asimovian directives, this terminator has been reprogrammed to protect John and Sarah at all costs, including his own destruction, he is consistently mistrusted largely *because* of his very look, with only his repeated efforts to put himself violently between the humans and a new sort of assassin terminator proving his dedication. But actions here ultimately prove more telling than appearances, suggesting that "humanity," however we want to define it, might be not some elusive essence but something we choose, something we construct day by day through behavior or choices. Because that other terminator is a newer model T-1000, a liquid metal shape-shifter able to look and sound like anyone—or anything—it samples, the film is able to generate an enhanced level of paranoia, one that attaches not simply to the overly large, extra-muscled, and menacingly dressed, such as Schwarzenegger's character, but to all appearances here (as, for example, when the T-1000 morphs from a checkered tile floor into various human shapes, ironically including that of a *security* guard). Tapping into state-of-the-art computer-generated imagery (CGI) effects provided by George Lucas' Industrial Light and Magic company, the film manages to suggest that nothing is what it seems and that nothing and no one can really be trusted—in fact, that reality itself, or at least its surfaces, has become just as unreliable as human, robotic, or, in an inevitable reflexive turn, even *cinematic* appearances.

That point is reiterated with a variety of complications in the subsequent feature films *Terminator 3: Rise of the Machines*, *Terminator Salvation*, and *Terminator Genisys*. In the first of these, the menacing terminator, now a T-X model, is given a superficially softer and more pleasing female identity, although it retains some of the T-1000's shape-shifter powers, as we see when, to avoid a policeman's interference as "she" chases John Connor and his girlfriend Kate, the T-X inflates its breasts to easily distract the officer. In this scene and elsewhere *Terminator 3* obviously begs questions about gender construction, warning against easy assumptions based on cultural stereotypes, while also deconstructing and commenting on the components of those stereotypes—in this case a slight build, blond hair, long legs, and exaggerated breasts, resulting as the narrative unfolds in several instances of what seems an almost absurd physical combat between two equally unrealistic yet culturally embraced physical types, a champion bodybuilder and a Barbie doll. Moreover, this T-X figure metaphorically plays upon that notion of seductive appearances that we previously observed in *Metropolis*, once again using it to suggest the tempting nature of technology itself, especially that which would seem to emphasize humanity's power.

With the more convoluted *Terminator Salvation* the seductive power of the skin job, along with its inevitable interrogation of gender roles and expectations, is subordinated to a complex pattern of unreliable appearances, all linked to the relationship between the mature John Connor and the part-cyborg Marcus Wright during the postapocalyptic human fight against Skynet and its various killing machines. Set in this war-devastated future, with few human structures or institutions to rely on, the narrative instead becomes fully focused on human images—and human trust. Connor must determine if he can rely on Wright, who was apparently intended to be the prototype for yet another sort of terminator, one that, in order to avoid detection by human sensors, combines real human flesh and organs with its machine parts. Meanwhile, Wright must cope with his own perception of himself as human—he looks in a mirror and sees himself as such—rather than machine, as well as with Skynet's perception that, because it has produced him, he *is* a machine. Guided by his sense that being partly human ultimately *makes* him human, and taking advantage of Skynet's *equally questionable* machinic understanding—that being partly machine makes him one with it—he manages to infiltrate its network and rescue key human prisoners held at Skynet headquarters. When John is subsequently mortally wounded in a Skynet trap—founded on this same complex web of calculated misperceptions—he and Wright find a point of compromise and conciliation, as the latter sacrifices one of his human components, his heart, for transplantation so that John can live and continue the fight against the supercomputer and its arsenal of other skin jobs. In that exchange and self-sacrifice, in doing something so intensely humane, of course, Marcus Wright recalls *Terminator 2*'s insistence that how one acts, not how one looks, is the real measure of one's humanity. With his sacrifice, Marcus affirms his fundamental humanity, just as does John Connor who draws on those problematic appearances—trusting in what cannot be immediately *seen*, such as Wright's heart—to gain new life for both himself and a humanity that is teetering on the edge of termination.

The most recent of these films, *Terminator Genisys*, offers a complex variation on the plot of the first two films in the series, with Kyle Reese again going back in time to "save" Sarah Connor from a time-traveling terminator. In this instance, though, it is Reese who must deal with a dazzling world of deceptive or unpredictable appearances and gender assumptions. Although John Connor warns Reese that Sarah will be "scared and weak," she proves to be anything but. In fact, in the film's beginning she has to save Reese from a liquid metal terminator that, just as in *Terminator 2*, has taken the form of a policeman, a figure who, despite appearances, aims not "to protect and serve" but to destroy. Driving right into a building where Reese is trapped, it is Sarah who holds off the terminator while offering Schwarzenegger's line from that film, "Come with me if you want to live!" (itself a reprise of Reese's line in the original *Terminator* film). As she then explains for both Reese and the audience, "Everything's changed," with the liquid metal terminator or T-1000 only serving as the most overt sign of the host of unreliable and unexpected images that the film's multiple, varied, and altered timelines have produced, including a robotic version of Skynet disguised as one of Connor's lieutenants and an image of John Connor himself that is not John Connor but rather a robot version, a new nanomachine model or T-3000 that has taken him over and must itself be "terminated" if the humans are to survive.

Early in the film a time-traveling, early-model T-800 terminator comes across a group of punks who marvel at this naked figure striding right up to them, as one offers, "What's wrong with this picture?" It is a question that might function thematically not only for this latest entry in the series, but indeed for all of the *Terminator* films, as all play with problematic images and suggest, with a large measure of contemporary paranoia, a fitting suspicion of how things seem. In the case of *Terminator Genisys* that interrogation is simply pushed to an extreme not seen in any of the prior films, because—abetted by the film's multiple time-travel events—there are different versions of characters, combat between two seemingly identical T-800 robots, shape-shifting robots, and even different sorts of shape-shifters (T-1000 and T-3000 models), as well as near-identical scenes from other entries in the series. But that constant weaving of sameness and difference creates a maze of troubling appearances that is symptomatic of the entire series' efforts to use the robot as a tool for diagnosing a common sense that there is indeed something "wrong" with the picture offered to us by modern technological society.

If these last *Terminator* films provide cold comfort in our confrontation with the robot problematic—despite momentary triumphs, they all leave us narratively caught up in Skynet/Genisys' persistent survival and ongoing plan of apocalyptic destruction and human eradication—they do dramatically and violently illustrate the danger implicit in these robots-who-look-just-like-us that a host of such films would take up. The various terminator types that emerge during the course of the series all have great physical powers, bioengineered enhancements over the human body, and both their on-board electronic brains and their constant access to the Skynet super-computer provide them with a formidable mind power. But it is their ability to mimic the human, and practically anything else, that seems to strike most fundamentally—or terminally—at our sense of self. In defying even the apparent truth of the mirror, these skin jobs foreground the contemporary anxiety of living in a world of simulacra, one that has been well described by cultural critics such as Jean Baudrillard and Paul Virilio. The latter perhaps most clearly defines the problem when he describes how our very sense of reality has fallen victim to the contemporary "mediatized" world, one in which humans seem to have lost the "capacity to say, describe, and inscribe reality" (*Lost* 24). In such an environment, as he offers, everything around us, including our fellow humans, seems increasingly confused with a pervasive "reality effect" (*Lost* 34)—an effect that our films, with their increasing access to digital technologies that enable them to convincingly conjure almost anything we might imagine, repeatedly mirror.

Pointing toward such a mirror effect, Virilio has observed how, thanks to "the sudden proliferation and the incessant multiplication of special effects" (*Lost* 21), we often feel as if we are actually walking through a movie or other media production, with everything, including ourselves, transformed into such effects, into electronic or cinematic facsimiles of real humans, acting out their lives in a kind of Potemkin village or along a Disneyesque Main Street, full of audioanimatronic figures. The skin job simply foregrounds this contemporary confusion by seeming to erase what we might term the digital divide, the boundary between the reel and the real, or, more accurately, between the robotic and the real self. Living with the threat of that erasure, devaluation, or simply constant confusion, we cannot help but find this version of the robot to be a most disturbing presence—not just a potential replacement for the self, as *R. U. R.* had ominously forecast, but a new measure of both the world and the self.

It is this notion of a possible new measure that seems to underlie one of the more significant sf television series of recent times, the rebooted

Battlestar Galactica (2004–09). Based on an earlier series of 1978–80 that detailed a human conflict with a robotic race, the Cylons who have similarly sought to terminate humanity, the new program has been widely lauded for its contemporary cultural analysis, especially its metaphoric replaying of the events of 9/11 and the subsequent war on terror. Framing such events in the context of rejuvenated hostilities not just with robots, but with robots who pointedly do not match up with the humans' previous conceptions of such figures, allows the newer *Battlestar Galactica* to foreground and better explore that relationship between appearance and action, and even to give a more nuanced vision of the seemingly inevitable conflicts between different races, different cultures, and different religions that are all implicated in those recent cultural events the series mirrors.

Preparatory to the series' launch, a three-hour miniseries detailed a new Cylon surprise attack on the various human colonies, introduced by emphasizing precisely that sense of human—and robotic—measure. In this reboot of the original series the Cylons are not simply an alien race but, as a title card explains, a machine species created by man "to make life easier" for humans. However, as in the ur-narrative *R. U. R.*, the *Terminator* saga, and various other robot stories, these servants, after becoming aware of their subaltern status, "decided to kill their masters." Following the Cylons' defeat, the humans, we are told, established a remote space station as a neutral site for contact and negotiations, but forty years of silence and Cylon absence followed. As the series opens, we see a human representative viewing the "technical specifications" of the Cylons—an image of the robots from the 1978–80 series—but perfunctorily, given the Cylons' long absence. But his detached attitude shatters when a door suddenly opens and two robots, who look nothing like the original Cylons, enter, flank the door, and then follow as a tall blond woman enters and approaches the human representative. Number Six, as she is identified in the series, is a very different breed of Cylon; wearing a tight red dress and brown suede boots, she is, as Susan George has observed, from the start "hypersexualized both in action and dress" (165) and every bit as much a visual challenge to the human representative as are the new-style robots who accompany her. What she represents is a new generation of Cylons, indistinguishable from the humans on which they are modeled, and as much a puzzle to the human representative as he seems to be to her—thus her initial words, "Are you alive?" which are followed by a challenge, "Prove it!" Both statements, much like her own unexpectedly "hypersexualized" image, immediately raise the issue of "measure," although shifting it from our usual concern solely with the human to a broader category of how we might measure life itself. In this new circumstance, the show announces, one where robots and humans seem indistinguishable, where robots and humans will increasingly interact (her sudden and passionate kissing of the human representative as a kind of "proof" forecasts a variety of intimate interspecies relationships throughout the series), and where both species will manifest the same sorts of feelings and attitudes, a new measure clearly seems needed. And with a new war beginning with a 9/11-like attack and all surfaces now suspect, actions alone will have to "prove" reliable and truthful.

Following this quite literal yet also thematic prologue, the series then details a complex web of human/Cylon relationships, as the human Dr. Gaius Baltar is seduced by a Number Six and betrays his fellow humans, as another Cylon, Number Eight or Athena, helps the humans defeat a Cylon attack, and as several of the most trusted humans prove either unreliable comrades or planted Cylon agents. Even the human president, Laura Roslin, finds at one point she must deal with mutineers among the human survivors, and at another make a peace pact with a group of Cylons who have similarly rebelled against their own leaders, all while she tries to lead a ragtag group of surviving humans to a "new" planet, Earth. By the series' final season, it is clear that both sides have committed the sorts of atrocities linked to the war on terror, although it is also often unclear who is truly human and who is a Cylon. The "sides" have simply blurred, and only the goodwill that many of these obviously "alive" entities manifest offers some hope for the future. The founding of a new Earth colony, and indeed the propagation of life itself, will require everyone to move beyond surfaces, whether of skin or metal, and embrace a common measure, that of life itself—a life particularly represented by the first offspring of a human–Cylon mating.

Figure 4.3 The new style Cylons of television's *Battlestar Galactica* (2004–09). Universal.

Perhaps it is that very disturbing confusion or blurring demonstrated by both the *Terminator* films and the *Battlestar Galactica* franchise that is responsible for what we might see as a curious element of fecundity, that is, a new and more complicated image pattern that has surfaced in a variety of such skin job texts. As an introductory example, we might consider a striking advertisement for another television series, the spin-off *Terminator: The Sarah Connor Chronicles* (2008–9). Recalling the disturbing image of the terminator's torso, partially destroyed but still threatening, doggedly creeping after an injured Sarah Connor in the concluding scene of the original *The Terminator*, this ad for the television show offers an image of the naked upper torso of a new terminator, but this one a young female, Cameron, played in obvious contrast to Arnold Schwarzenegger's outsized and formidable figure by the slightly built Summer Glau. Although the image seems at least partly intended to capitalize in a very immediate way on Glau's seductive attributes by objectifying her and her nudity—her status as a kind of robot remnant seemingly *permitting* our gaze—it also speaks to another dimension of this figure. That upper torso, suspended by wires and cables, with other wires, cables, tubing, and metal armature hanging down from her insides, clearly marks her as a partially assembled—or disassembled—*thing*, as *not* human. And yet that image is arresting, not simply in a perversely gendered way, as another instance of a cultural tendency to fetishize and objectify elements of the female body, but as a trace of what Jane Bennett in her "ecology of things" describes as "thingly power, the material agency of natural bodies and technological artifacts" (*Vibrant* xiii).

Figure 4.4 The partial skin job as alluring ad: Cameron (Summer Glau) in *Terminator: The Sarah Connor Chronicles* (2008–9).

Lorrie Palmer has observed how throughout the run of *Terminator: The Sarah Connor Chronicles*, the Cameron character is portrayed as one who takes pains to look, dress, and act quite ordinarily, constantly working at—and talking about—"blending in" (87) or passing for a typical teenager so that she can better do the job she has been programmed for: to protect the real teenager, John, from possible time-traveling assassins. However, the ad promotes both character and series by inviting us to see her not as some "typical teenager," but rather as a "technological artifact," because it shows us what underlies her "outwardly typical high-school girl" appearance (88), namely, all the inner workings of her constructed cyborg body. In permitting that view of both "skin" and mechanism, the ad does something more than offer a vision of conflicted desires, conflating the female and technology after the pattern of *Metropolis* and its prototype skin job; it lets us in on the trick, makes us aware of what lies beneath, revealing what is real and what is, after all, just a technologically fashioned "reality effect," as Virilio would say. Although this version of the human, as we clearly see, is indeed only skin deep and perhaps not quite the metaphysical challenge—or seductive lure—it might initially appear to be, in its very thing-ness it does evoke another sort of challenge, as Bennett offers, "how to acknowledge the obscure but ubiquitous intensity of impersonal affect" (*Vibrant* xiii), that is, how do we explain the impact of such *things* on us? What is their "measure"?

This strange hybrid image, of the skin job reassuringly—if a bit messily—revealed, functions as a deliberate come-on or appeal for the series, and one that has found a level of persistence and complication that needs unpacking as we further explore this robot's ecology and the powerful relation it evokes between the self and the thing.[3] The Cameron-terminator-torso is just one in a long line of such revealed, partial, and objectified figures, usually female and often set in comparison to other skin jobs and used as a gloss on their appearance, appeal, and function—much as the opened-up tin-can robots of an earlier era afforded a kind of demystification of that model's mechanical power and uncanny appearance. Following the gender trail of this linkage of torso and appealing female body, Kevin Kelly has suggested that the *Terminator: The Sarah Connor Chronicles* ad was really little more than a gender ploy, a simple effort at capitalizing on similarly sexualized images found elsewhere, especially the cyborg torso featured in Mamoru Oshii's anime feature *Ghost in the Shell* (1995). In one of that film's more striking scenes, we witness government operatives inspecting and eventually trying to interrogate the upper remains of a naked female cyborg body, similarly dangling from wires and trailing its mechanical entrails. These government agents have been fighting against an elusive criminal figure, the Puppet Master, who had recently hacked into this synthetic female body in its original full form, animated it as an avatar, and then, after it was partially destroyed, continued to use it as a tool, talking through it—in a male voice—and mocking the futile human efforts at capturing him/her/it—the guiding intelligence behind, and ultimately separate from, the body. Kelly also suggests conceptual links to several other gendered variations on this striking figure, such as in Francis Ford Coppola's Disney theme park short *Captain Eo* (1986) and in the feature film *Star Trek: First Contact* (1996). In the former it takes the shape of the Supreme Leader of a mysterious planet, a woman suspended by and bound up in wires, cables, and tubes, obviously largely machinic herself, who is finally rendered fully human and even radiant by the transformative—and redemptive—music and dance/ actions of Michael Jackson's Captain Eo. In the latter it is the Borg Queen, leader of a race of cybernetic beings, whose upper torso we see being fitted into a lower machine body, and whose constructed race is presented as a kind of ultimate threat to humanity. In each case the narrative lingers on that striking torso image, capitalizing on its strange, fetishistic presentation of the feminine. But in that lingering, fascinated view, the figure also takes on, as noted earlier, a more than gendered power. Its sheer partiality, its manifest constructedness, and its uncanny vitality—"alive" in its own fashion, even when reduced to such a partial form—and all accompanied by an antagonism to humans, become clearly disconcerting characteristics, challenges to our normal categories of being that have typically been seen as implicit in these skin job creations.

Yet rather than marking a simple hierarchy of beings—composed of humans, cyborgs, and partial-yet-still-animate cyborgs—these figures might well be read, as Jane Bennett offers in another context, "horizontally as a juxtaposition rather than vertically" (*Vibrant* 9–10). When seen in this

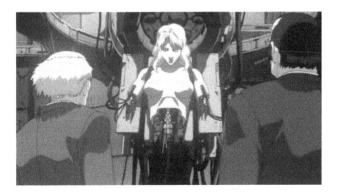

Figure 4.5 Interrogating the Puppet Master in *Ghost in the Shell* (1995). Shochiku.

way, they begin to suggest some of the ecological scope of the skin job, and also to explain at least some of the dis-ease it evokes. Signs of both an alien and object-like life form, cyborg and lifelike torso point to a continuity in which we might well include the human as well as other seemingly life-less objects—and thus a continuity in which subject and object all easily blur together, arguing for an unexpected kinship. Thus, despite that sense of dis-ease, both cyborg and torso retain a fascination for the characters in these stories, in part simply because humans seem to have played a crucial hand in their creation, but also in part because they do manifest a very different manner or level of vitality or vibrancy than we are familiar with or even able to measure, as if opening onto an unexpected kinship—much like that finally recognized by the humans and Cylons of *Battlestar Galactica*.

This relationship—whether seen as humanity's fault, feat, or future—and this figure's uncanny character are particularly underscored in some of the animate torso's other cinematic appearances. I want to focus particularly on several entries in the tellingly titled *Alien* film series, giving special attention to the first two of these films, *Alien* (1979) and *Aliens* (1986), as well as to director Ridley Scott's attempt to bind up the series in the more recent *Prometheus* (2012), as these three examples provide exemplary alternate visions of the nature and function of such partial skin jobs. All of these films about interstellar exploration and commerce include in their crews of space explorers/exploiters special android assistants, skin jobs, who, save when they pointedly demonstrate their special enhancements—superior strength, speed, memory—are visually indistinguishable from their human crewmates. Ash of *Alien* is, in fact, an android who has completely passed as the cargo ship *Nostromo*'s science officer. Secretly programmed by the sponsoring company to help bring back any alien specimens his ship encounters, even if doing so requires sacrificing the human crew, Ash is clearly unconstrained—and untroubled—by any Asimovian controls. Thus when the *Nostromo*'s Warrant Officer Ripley plots to destroy a deadly alien specimen that Ash, in defiance of protocols, has helped bring on board the *Nostromo*, he attempts to kill her. In the ensuing struggle, played as a sort of perverse rape in which he attacks her with a rolled up pornographic magazine, he is eventually dismembered, reduced to shoulders and a head—the prototype partial torso—and only at that point is he finally—and to the crew's amazement—identified as nonhuman. As one crew member notes in surprise, "Ash is a goddamned robot!" Yet even in that damned and decapitated form, with his insides scattered outside and all over the deck and partially covered in a thick white liquid that his body oozes, he is reanimated, interrogated, and, before being destroyed, proceeds to taunt Ripley and the others, assuring them that they cannot possibly survive against such a "perfect" killing machine as this alien species. In this horrific form and lacking what Ximena Gallardo and Jason Smith describe as the sort of "moral and ethical imperatives by which humanity attempts to define itself" (51), Ash easily seems as "alien" as this predatory form that is gradually killing off the crew and with which he apparently recognizes some kinship.

In the sequel *Aliens* a similar torso role is filled by Bishop, another android assistant on a deep-space mission, although in this instance everyone on the ship is well aware of his "difference," of his status as a "technological arti-fact." Building on that awareness, director James Cameron shifts attention from the possible threat of the robot to the demonstration of all-too-familiar human prejudices and suspicions of the "Other" or alien, with the crew members treating Bishop as something very different—not as another crew member, but rather as a living curiosity, a sophisticated tool, or, in the case of Ripley, whose attitude is colored by her previous experience with Ash, as a figure of both disdain and distrust. Yet in contrast to Ash, Bishop is indeed bound by those Asimovian rules that ensure human protection and even though during the film's final confrontation with the alien queen he is torn in half and thus also reduced to a living torso, he continues to aid the surviving humans. A more complex figure than Ash, Bishop is fully aware that he is something both more and *less* than human; in fact, thanks to the crew's reactions to him, he *lives* that sense of difference every day, as when they ask him to perform a trick with a knife, as if he were just a machine or trained animal. However, in his reactions, self-consciousness, and judgment he also seems to suggest that *how* he is both more and less than human can-not be so easily measured by either the skin or those unfamiliar bits, pieces, and goo we eventually see spilling out from his torso. Although we view his various parts, *know* that he is a constructed thing, his behavior and *actions*, in contrast to those of Ash, argue—as, after a fashion, all of these torsos

Figure 4.6 Reduced to a living torso: the partial skin job Bishop (Lance Henriksen) of *Aliens* (1986). 20th Century Fox.

do—that we reconsider what constitutes the category of the human and, ultimately, how we define the alien or Other.

Although Bishop's remains would reappear in *Alien³* (1992) and another, even more pointedly self-conscious and insecure skin job, Call, would play a central role in a fourth entry in the series, *Alien Resurrection* (1997), the most telling link to and significant development from the first two films is probably the android character found in Ridley Scott's *Prometheus*. That film's David, who is also a kind of all-purpose assistant to an expedition sent to locate the suspected origins of humanity on a distant moon, seems torn between his programming, which, as with Ash, directs him to support the space mission at all costs—even human costs—and his own curiosity about and even seeming sympathies for a larger category, as in *Battlestar Galactica*, for life itself. Ostensibly, this deep-space mission is aimed at locating the Engineers, as they are termed, those thought to have originally created humanity, seeding them on Earth. However, this mission's deeper and hidden purpose, and the one that David secretly aids, is to communicate with the Engineers and convince them to provide the expedition's aged sponsor, wealthy industrialist Peter Weyland, with extended life—in effect, to make him *unlike* any other human, functionally *alien*. Working somewhat like Ash, then, David secretly "engineers" a new sort of life by contaminating with alien bacteria the drink of Holloway, another crew member, who then impregnates the archeologist Elizabeth Shaw. As he later tries to communicate with a surviving Engineer, however, David, just like his android predecessors, is ripped apart, reduced to a still-living head and shoulders, and, like Bishop, David as living torso eventually helps Shaw escape from that Engineer figure whose mission, it seems, was to unleash a life-extinguishing plague on Earth. The film ends with Shaw, accompanied and partly guided by David's still conscious remains, leaving the moon in search of the Engineers' home planet and, with it, explanations for both humanity's origins and the Engineers' strange desire to put an end to the human life they had originated—explanations that we might assume to be forthcoming in the planned sequel to the film, the allusively but tentatively titled *Paradise*.

Just as much as the skin jobs that they begin as, these various torsos or remains, these almost equally persistent images, seem a significant component of the robotic ecology sketched here. As our earlier "horizontal" reading suggested, they foreground an easy slippage between living being and thing, in the process pointing to a disconcerting connection between the two. Moreover, they almost literally demonstrate what Nicholas Mirzoeff, in his discussion of the role of the human body in Western art, has described as an abiding and intriguing "tension between the perfect and fragmentary body . . . expressed in a new form: the fragmentary and transitory glimpse of the perfect body before its inevitable destruction" (172). That foreboding about an "inevitable" destruction and the "tension" attending the different forms and states of the body give reason to that being/thing relationship that seems surprisingly implicit in this version of the skin job robot.

As Mirzoeff has further argued, the tension that he identifies actually reflects a body "crisis" long simmering in Western culture. This body tension, he suggests, has followed from a variety of ideological and cultural crises, all of which have left us with an "alarming feeling of instability" (2) and a tendency in art and popular culture to project "a palpable sense of dis-ease about the bodyscape" (3). The result is a trend in both modern and postmodern art and culture to examine this troubled state by depicting the body in duress, as embattled, fragmented, torn in different directions, as if ready to shift into object-hood—a depiction perhaps most obvious in Marcel Duchamp's Cubist-style paintings, but also readily visible in Barbara Kruger's photomontages of cut-up personal images and text, the performance artist Orlan's various reconfiguring plastic surgeries on herself as she sculpts her body in bizarre ways, or even Morgan Spurlock's presentation of the self as a site of radical dietary experimentation in his "documentary" *Super Size Me* (2004). Seen from this vantage, all become quite literally versions of the robotic skin job as they map out the images of ideological, cultural, and personal fragmentation and dis-ease on the modern body.

In their own "transitory" moment, the robotic figures we find in *Alien*, *Aliens*, and *Prometheus* also verge on this sort of presentation with their visions of the fragmented human body and a persistently embattled sense of self—a self that always seems on the verge of alien-ness. For, on the one hand, as in the long visual tradition that Mirzoeff chronicles, these androids are striking emblems of what we might accomplish, of the human desire and ability to fashion nearly perfect simulacra, even to *become* perfect. *Prometheus'* David, for example, readily recalls Michelangelo's *David* and that statue's famed depiction of supposed anatomic perfection. But on the other hand, these figures' partial, torn, yet still functional remains serve to mock both aim and accomplishment, pointing up the fragmented, unstable human image we would prefer to overlook, to ascribe to a fantasized female gender, or to project onto an abject Other, such as the visceral, biomechanical alien figure famously conjured up by H. R. Giger for these films.[4] They thus serve to remind us—in the absence of intercession from something like *Prometheus*'s originary Engineers—of our own fleeting nature, our "inevitable" nearness to object-hood.

Moreover, these androids also provide an interesting commentary on the robot's visual challenge, on the power of that technological bodyscape that was first demonstrated in *Metropolis*. In showing us what moves beneath those trompe-l'oeil surfaces that these figures deploy so effectively—and in the case of Ash, deceptively—the torn and partial torsos we have been describing let us clearly see, despite all appearances, despite the very convincing nature of the androids and our usual human-centric ways of measuring worth, and even despite what is apparently a natural human tendency, as scientists have observed, to respond to the robotic "as a living thing" (Young), that they are just put-together objects and ultimately less or other than human. Of course, that insight is finally not very comforting, because even when faced with their brokenness, we are still haunted by those seeming perfections that these narratives so often demonstrate: not just the superficial aesthetic perfection of a David, but these robots' prodigious onboard information/intelligence; far superior strength; machine-like precision; untiring, relentless activity; and the ease with which they manage to pass for human—but especially their actions. Somehow, all that we see fails to explain all that we see, especially the very different sorts of conduct observed in figures like Ash, Bishop, and David. All are self-conscious, all show at least moments of sympathy for and/or curiosity about their human companions, and David particularly, even as the partial and lingering technological life form that he is reduced to at the end of *Prometheus*, seems every bit as much interested in pursuing the answers about life as does Shaw's committed archeologist. In this context we might recall how little was revealed—or learned—when one opened up the tin can robots encountered in such films as *The Phantom Empire* and *Undersea Kingdom*; the vision of gears and pulleys, of clockwork parts and radio receivers, eventually explained little about their own semblance of life. It is the same point we earlier noted in our discussion of that most influential of robot works, Capek's *R. U. R.*, wherein visitors to the robot factory are shown the efficient inner workings of a robot only to learn that there is surprisingly "not much in it." Similarly, at least in the *Alien* family of films, neither skin nor the bits and pieces tell the whole story, and that insistent pairing—of the skin job and its torn torso—seems every bit as troubling and challenging as the robot's simple, "perfect" ability to pass.

To consider part of what escapes our understanding even as the robot's phenomenal nature persists in the sf imagination, we might return briefly to *Terminator: The Sarah Connor Chronicles*, and particularly to that ad wherein, despite her partial status, as torso, Cameron's eyes pointedly engage our own, as if she were already or still—and pointedly we cannot know which—alive. That look of outward regard, combined with her/its ambiguous state (which could fit into the category of *not yet* or *no longer* alive), produces an uncanny effect that, as recent discussions of robotic creations have emphasized, seems to remain one of the more disconcerting properties of the skin job—in both fact and film. In 1970 the Japanese robotics scientist Masahiro Mori observed that as robots take on ever more human-like appearances, they trigger a disconcerting emotional response in human observers—an effect for which he coined the term "uncanny valley," suggesting the possibly unbridgeable chasm marking our inability to feel a true "affinity" for them (Mori), or, I might suggest, the sort of psychic abyss into which we sense we might be plunged should we make that commitment of human identification or empathetic reaction.

In either case, the impression that the humanoid robot is *like* a human but, in some eerie and almost intangible way, not quite *right* produces a negative feeling, even a kind of "creepiness," as Mori puts it. In efforts at explaining this common reaction, some have simply linked it to the Freudian death impulse or to intimations of our own mortality—implications that seem to readily fit with the thrust of the various *Alien* films, with the many texts and cultural alarms about robots replacing humanity (as dramatized in *R. U. R.*), as well as with the intimations of object-hood we have noted. To forestall engaging that uncanny effect, Mori has suggested that robot designers might problematize their designs in various ways, for example, by aiming for only "a moderate degree of human likeness" (Mori) in their creations. Recently, roboticists working with more human-seeming skin jobs have tried to address this problem not by caricature, but by generally concentrating their efforts on androids that serve only very simple human functions and that interact with humans on a basic informational level—such as android receptionists, newsreaders, and museum guides, that is, as human *types* that we customarily interact with in a kind of automatic, machinic, nearly invisible fashion, ones whose not-rightness we might hardly even notice and more easily overlook—much as we already seem to do the humanity of many of those we briefly encounter or interact with every day.[5] This approach, however, only disguises the actual problem, delaying the real confrontation that is implicit in the skin job and that our films tend to drive home.

In fact, with the fecund pairings of perfect and partial robots presented by our sf film and television texts, we practically have to notice. Even if these advanced androids' ability to pass somehow circumvented that uncanny effect, then their torn yet still-living torsos, a bit paradoxically, fully mobilize it. Earlier we noted how Cameron consistently tries to blend in, to avoid notice, as if despite her generally attractive appearance she cannot mask that surplus sense of the not-quite-right—a sense that Summer Glau had previously honed in her portrayal of the government brainwashed and dangerously programmed robot-like River Tam of the *Firefly* (2002–3) television series and its film sequel *Serenity* (2005). Throughout *The Sarah Connor Chronicles* series we are consistently reminded that, despite her slight appearance, Cameron is not what she seems. Like River, she is quite dangerous; she is, after all, a terminator who has been reprogrammed, her artificial intelligence grafted onto the identity of a resistance fighter of the future. As a result, she always—and in another sort of surplus sense—embodies a tension between her machinic and human selves, with her very "creepiness" serving as a sign of her constant potential to explode into violent action to protect Sarah and John, or even to revert to her original state and turn on them. In drawing that uncanny experience so near the surface, even foregrounding it, this series practically requires that we look beyond skin and parts, surface and depth, and that we match them up with the robot's actions—in short, that we consider a kind of ethics implicit in the workings of this simulacrum, this not-quite-human thing, this obviously "vibrant matter," as Jane Bennett might describe it/her (*Vibrant* 112).

Certainly that seems to be the pattern mapped out in the whole family of *Alien* films. Ash proves himself every bit as deadly and lacking in compunction as the biomechanoid alien he has abetted—or the invisible corporate entity he serves; Bishop struggles at all costs to help his human companions survive; and David joins Shaw in following a most fundamental human programming—a search for meaning, but particularly the meaning of life itself. Surfaces—or skin—as these characters all variously attest, are useful, disguising difference, allowing for interaction, even encouraging empathy—up to a point. Seen in this light, the different skin jobs we have surveyed present themselves as a version of what Darko Suvin has termed the "necessary and sufficient conditions" of all sf: "the presence and interaction of estrangement and cognition" (7)—or of the uncanny and the familiar. However, their likeness to the human, their visual appeal, these films all warn, just like *Metropolis* long before them, should not seduce us. For the skin jobs only approach, or depart from, humanity insofar as they are able to act in humane ways, and that is the measure or model that they— in the best tradition of the sf film—hold up for our inspection and, in those best instances, our imitation.

Ultimately, the lengthy popularity of this particular version of the cinematic robot, of the skin job, as I have termed it, is not really tied to an anxiety about our own looks but about our actions—or, more precisely, how we might act in a world thoroughly saturated with and conditioned by technology, a world in which objects have become disturbingly like subjects, a world where we are not the only "perfect" images. This point is at the heart of a more recent film like *Avatar* (2009), in which a crippled human, his mind downloaded into that of a nine-foot tall, blue-skinned humanoid, eventually comes to embrace that very different-looking alternate identity as he comes to sympathize with the actions of this species rather than their human exploiters. All of these persistent versions of the robot commonly underscore how, at least in the modern era, our very concept of the human is itself constantly being constructed and reconstructed—perhaps necessarily so—*through* our relationship to that pervasive technology of artifice. And the tales of science and technology that we repeatedly tell, particularly through the science and technology–empowered vehicle of the cinema, speak powerfully about the rising anxieties we feel in the face of that constructedness—in the face of a danger that ultimately strikes at our sense of self, or as Virilio puts it, "a disturbance in self-perception that will have lasting effects on man's rapport with the real" (*Art* 147). The skin job may well be the most threatening, most nearly perfect challenge to that self-perception. If it can act in human ways—or, as *Avatar* suggests, even more humanely, perhaps not such a difficult trick after all, given our histories of war, genocide, and self-destruction—then that uncanny gaze it (or its torso partner) fixes on us might stand as a suggestion that, today, the humans are the ones who are not quite right. And that gaze, that cinematic look of outward regard, might, in this case, serve a significant corrective function.

Turning reality into simply another "effect," no more real than the "special effects" that drive all of the films discussed here, gives some reason to this persistent figure of the robot, reminding us of how much this image, in all of the forms we have noted, is tied into the very appeal of the sf genre and into what we have termed the sf imagination. But although an economic imperative might have impelled much of the persistence that marked the reuse of some earlier versions of the robot, particularly the tin can types on which we initially focused—those whose costumes were readily available to movie studios and cheap—it is clearly not the driving force in our more recent robotic images. The appeal of those that look like us and whose only robotic giveaways, such as partially exposed metallic skeletons, adjustable eyes, transformable parts, etc., are typically the products of makeup, prosthetics, and the new regime of digital imagery—a regime that could easily and even with some economy create *any* sort of robotic image we might desire—is obviously different. With these figures, that persistence is all the more clearly linked to a cultural imaginary that has found the sf genre to be one of the key narrative formulas of today, and an imaginary that is especially haunted by the implications of what has, almost from sf cinema's origins, proven to be one of its most compelling images.

In the course of this discussion we have now surveyed three persistent visions of the robot—persistent at least in the American sf cinema and popular media that have produced more such robot narratives than any other national media. But the last of these types, the skin job, given the length of its popularity and the ease with which it allows the human image itself to function as a metaphor, a challenge, or even a corrective is probably the most telling of all. For it suggests a sense that we might already at some level be colluding in the roboticization, even replacement, that so many of these films forecast, accepting, or at least struggling with, our own place amid a world of increasing "reality effects," contributing to—and contending with—the ongoing construction of a world inhabited by what we today term posthumans. Although that sense of possible replacement obviously retains its alarming capacity, the possibility of an ethical awakening, keyed to a more vital sense of our place in the world, holds a real attraction. Seen in such lights, the thing-that-looks-like-us, the skin job, the human-seeming robot represents no puzzle as the latest and most persistent inheritor of the robot image in our cinematic consciousness. For it reminds us that, especially today, it is our own quite dangerous—and possibly fleeting—image that we see so clearly in the mirror of the movies and our other popular media. Across a variety of manifestations, the skin job—like its other persistent robotic representations of earlier days and in the best tradition of the sf imagination—offers us a useful way of contemplating, better understanding, and perhaps accommodating our visions of the old *and* a new self.

Notes

1 As just one example preceding *Metropolis*, we might point to the early Mack Sennett comedy *A Clever Dummy* (1917) in which Ben Turpin plays both a janitor and a robot modeled on him.

2 The distinctions that most would point to designate the android as a human-looking yet mechanical being, the cyborg as an amalgam of human and machine or biological and machinic elements, and the replicant as an artificially "grown" or fashioned being, usually having advanced capacities, such as sight, hearing, or physical strength.

3 Another dimension of this hybridity seems worth noting, because it points to a further dimension of fecundity at work in the case of these skin job figures. Because of their box office success, the *Terminator* films have spawned a great variety of toys. However, the television series, because it lasted only two seasons, did not produce a similar product line. As a result, fans have taken to creating their own action figures and vehicles through a hybrid activity termed "toy bashing" or "kit bashing"—a practice that involves putting together pieces from other toys or model kits and then sculpting and painting them to resemble the desired toy line. For discussion and examples of this practice, see Chris Vanne's "Action Figures of Cameron in TSCC" on the Summer Glau fansite.

4 For his work in *Alien*—as well as his inspiration to other films in the series—Giger received an Academy Award for Visual Effects and was in 2013 elected to the Science Fiction and Fantasy Hall of Fame. His pointedly hybrid biomechanical figures not only suggest a linkage to the skin jobs discussed here—as if they are skin jobs turned inside out—but also externalize the threat sensed in such constructed figures.

5 Appropriately, several such figures have been introduced to serve in Tokyo's National Museum of Emerging Science. "Making androids is about exploring what it means to be human," offers robot creator Hiroshi Ishiguro, as he introduced two silicon-skinned robots, one designed to read daily news reports, like a television news anchor, and the other to serve as a guide at the Tokyo National Museum in 2014.

5   The Self in Tomorrowland

Early in the iconic sf film *Star Wars* (aka *A New Hope*, 1977), the anthropo-morphic robot C-3P0 finds himself rescued (or captured, depending on one's perspective) by a group of Jawas and dumped into their sand rover's storage compartment, which contains an array of other mechanical figures they have collected. Some are vaguely familiar—such as the maintenance robots from *Silent Running* (1972)—and underscore the film's pattern of homages to the variety of its generic predecessors. Others are simply strange, alien looking, even comic in aspect, but all register as vaguely threating to a very proper "protocol" 'droid like C-3P0, who does not seem to recognize that they are all part of the same "species." However, their very variety is noteworthy, because it points to the many types of robots that have been conceived and fashioned by the various cultures and creatures inhabiting this "galaxy far, far away" from our own, even as it also suggests the great diversity of such creations that the sf film has, over its own long history, conjured up for our consideration. It is a diversity that has partly been pushed to the periphery of this discussion, as we have tried to sketch not so much a history of the form as an ecology, and thus to focus on dominant patterns instead of specific versions. Yet that variety is part of the larger background, the texture of this study, largely because it indicates the promise of both the robot and the cin-ema, their congruent abilities and persistent efforts at visualizing whatever shape, function, or cognitive level we might desire from our technology.

More pointedly, *Star Wars'* image of great variety—further emphasized by its friendship between an almost literal tin can, R2-D2, and the highly anthropomorphic C-3PO—amply testifies to what we have termed the fecundity of this conception, the robot's ability to suggest other construc-tions of the mechanical being, both in a particular era and across practi-cally the whole history of film. It has become, as the introduction suggested, one of the most iconic emblems of the sf film—indeed, perhaps the most iconic. And appropriately so, because the figure of the robot links the film medium's fundamental fascination with exploring the human image—and in this context we might recall Bela Balazs' early assessment that film's own power and appeal were primarily lodged in its "mighty visual anthropomorphism" (60)—with the film genre's constant efforts at taking the measure of humanity, particularly in terms of its relationship to science and technology. That variety of images, in fact, points to those repeated—and, as a spate of recent films like *Ex Machina*, *Terminator Genisys*, *Chappie*, and *Tomorrowland* (all 2015) indicate, ongoing—measures as we try to visualize how technology might affect a number of the most pressing human issues: our notions of gender (*Ex Machina*), identity (*Terminator*), the family (*Chappie*), even human survival (*Tomorrowland*). But such efforts have always been the strength of the sf genre and a sign of the imagination that powers it. And this strength is one of the reasons that, as recent decades have made most obvious, it has spread itself so effectively across a broad media spectrum, becoming a dominant generic influence not only in film, but also in television, comics, and video games.

That sense of variety might also remind us of something that, although not quite missing from our focus here on three dominant robotic memes, has perhaps been overshadowed. As has been observed by Vivian Sobchack, one of the form's most influential commentators, sf, unlike many other film genres, often seems to slide away from a "consistent cluster of meanings provoked by" its icons (5). Whether we consider the futuristic city, the spaceship, or, in this instance, the robot, we frequently face, as she suggests, a pattern of "fluctuating meanings" that she believes is due largely to the nature of the genre: its "plasticity of objects and settings" that stands in marked contrast to what she calls "the essentially static worlds of genres such as the western and gangster film" (10). Although her argument on the basis of sf's relative freedom from "temporality" (that is, its ability to imagine *any* time) might be open to debate, her larger assessment, that sf often

Figure 5.1 Luke Skywalker (Mark Hamill) examines a range of robots for sale in *Star Wars* (1977). 20th Century Fox.

plunges commentators into "more ambiguous territory" (10) than other genres, seems especially pertinent here. For even as we have throughout this work emphasized the persistence of certain robotic memes and suggested some rather obvious essentialist implications that typically attach to those memes—such as the machinic power and behavior that marked our early tin can robots—we have also observed the frequently shifting character of those same memes, as when Robby the Robot, in various closely clustered episodes of *The Twilight Zone*, becomes emblematic of a modern child's plaything, the pressing threat of automation, and the oppressive potential of artificial intelligence—or when a tin can, over time, gains strength, intelligence, and even a human appearance. Variety, even within certain persistent memes, it seems, is not only to be expected, but also is a part of the genre's strength and strategy.

In this context I would like to briefly consider one of those recent robot films, *Tomorrowland*, to consider how it offers its own vision of such variety and "fluctuating meanings," even while it largely anchors its robotic vision in the skin job type. Early in the film its protagonist, the precocious teenager Casey, comes to an sf memorabilia shop full of robot replicas that recall the diverse collection noted in the scene from *Star Wars*. A by no means complete list of the robots glimpsed in either model or full-size mock-up form in this scene includes Gort from *The Day the Earth Stood Still*, Robby of *Forbidden Planet*, Robot B-9 from *Lost in Space*, R2-D2 of the *Star Wars* films, and, as director Brad Bird's self-homage to his first film, the title figure from his *The Iron Giant* (1999). This jumble of various models and replicas, along with a number of film poster images, readily suggests what a prominent role the robot has played in our media history, as well as its ongoing appeal. In this instance, these figures are all being offered as collectibles and toys by a strangely mismatched couple, seemingly the stereotypical eccentric sf nerds. Surprisingly, though, they turn out to be robots themselves, and ones that quickly shift character, and thus "meaning," from simple shopkeepers to menacing figures who first threaten Casey in order to learn how much she knows about the futuristic world dubbed Tomorrowland, and then try to kill her.

The robotic couple's rapid and radical fluctuations of identity only serve to introduce the multiple nature of the robots we encounter throughout this film. As these and a host of others that soon begin chasing Casey violently demonstrate, the robots that have been fashioned in the alternate realm of Tomorrowland can be relentless and deadly, and they are unrestrained by any Asimovian compunctions. Yet another robot, the aptly named Athena who looks like a preadolescent girl, shows a further dimension of these figures, that some of them can be wise, caring, and protective of humans. The robots of Tomorrowland can also look very much like Robby the Robot,

Figure 5.2 The robot shop owners—and sellers of robot memorabilia—from
Tomorrowland (2015). Disney.

as we see when Governor Nix employs several monstrous metal robots to capture Athena and her human companions, Casey and Frank Walker. However, Athena, as we see in a flashback when a younger Frank tries to confess his rather obvious love for her, is herself beautiful, capable of feeling and expressing a full range of emotions, and is ultimately indistinguishable from a human. Moreover, Athena repeatedly demonstrates a mind of her own—a *wisdom* in keeping with her name—that distinguishes her from the relentless and threatening robots who pursue their quarry at all costs and with great destructive, even self-destructive, effects, as they try to stop her and Frank. But the varying looks, functions, and capacities of these constructed beings only underscore, for both this narrative and the larger canon of the sf film, the multiple potentials that we commonly attach to such creations—even the multiple hopes for both the present and "tomorrow" that we always seem to lodge in these projections of the human—here a hope that, as Frank spells out, we might use them to help us somehow "fix the future."

Those hopes also give some reason for the ongoing appeal of such figures and, as we have several times noted, the central or "starring" place they have often taken in our sf cinema. In the previous chapter we noted the uncanny effect that frequently attaches to the robot, both in the cinema and in real life. As we exchange glances with such figures, we feel not a sense of commonness, of shared humanity, but rather a distance—or "valley," as those in the sciences have dubbed it—as human and thing are suddenly and uncomfortably linked ontologically. Put more simply, it is a sense of unease, even a kind of alienation that we feel—one all the more disturbing because at times we cannot be sure whether it is us or the robot that seems the alien, the figure that, our senses tell us, is out of place here. That sensation should give us some pause as we consider the appeal of the robot across its many different manifestations, including the three dominant formulations on which we have here focused.

In her own ecological study of "things," a category in which many would quickly place the robot, Jane Bennett points us in a useful direction. She describes a much broader uncanny feeling, a pattern of "disenchantment" (*Enchantment* 3) that she believes has descended on the contemporary world, thanks largely to our efforts at deploying a rational and human-centric attitude that establishes our role as that of the world's knower and master—outside of and beyond all the things of this world[1]—even as it also places us at a great distance from everything that constitutes this world. And yet, as she notes, "surprises . . . regularly punctuate life" (3), especially when we encounter things that do not succumb to cold logic, that we cannot easily explain or fully "know," that frustrate or counter that sense of detachment. Thus Bennett describes a wide variety of ways in which "enchantment" still exercises a powerful influence on humans, allowing us "to be struck and shaken by the extraordinary" that we often accidentally or unexpectedly encounter (*Enchantment* 40), much as the young Frank, while attending the 1964 New York World's Fair, accidentally encountered and found himself fully enchanted by the charming Athena, who first offered him the hopeful message that "nothing is impossible" and who has similarly tantalized Casey with that optimistic notion.

The robot exercises such an attraction for us in large part because it remains one of those "extraordinary" things—in fact, a figure that, rather *enchantingly*, can remind us of the peculiar vitality of things, or what Bennett terms the "vibrant matter" (*Vibrant* viii) that is actually all around us, waiting to be noticed. Although constructed from the elements of that world, although conjured by the combined forces of reason, science, and technology—the triad on which all sf stands—the robot still confronts us with a kind of limit of understanding, and in doing so serves not just as a brake on the elements of that triad, but as a spur to their development as well, as it helps to satisfy one of the essential—and most important— functions of the sf imagination, its ability to meet what Michele Pierson, following a number of other commentators, terms our "cultural demand for the aesthetic experience of wonder" (168).

To better see how that "demand" might be satisfied by this figure, we might consider the experience of wonder at work in another of these recent robot films, Alex Garland's *Ex Machina*, a movie that is in great part about the seductive appeal that such figures can wield. Much as in *Tomorrowland*, *Ex Machina* offers us not one robot type, but several different visions of this figure: a to-all-appearances human Kyoko, introduced as electronics genius Nathan Bateman's Japanese maid, although strangely for a servant, she seems to have no language capability at all; a long closet full of metal and tube skeletons, some with partial "skin" coverings or wigs, which Nathan describes as early robot prototypes that he has over the years developed and then junked; and Ava, his most recent creation, whose body is partly skin-covered and partly encased in plastic, allowing us to see the various wires, tubes, and actuators inside her, as if we were looking into one of those tin can figures, just as Gene Autry and Crash Corrigan once did. But as Nathan confides to his employee Caleb, Ava differs from his earlier creations because of her advanced artificial intelligence. In fact, she is so advanced that he wants Caleb to help him put "her" to a version of the famous Turing Test, to see if one can tell whether she is human *not* by looking at—or into—her, but by interacting with her linguistically and even emotionally as he subtly induces Caleb into doing. The spectacle confronting Caleb, of a kind of technological half-breed, already suggests that there is something amiss in this test, because it confronts him with certain unavoidable visual facts in a way that the theoretical Turing Test would never have done.[2] Ava is a figure that, in her face and some parts of her body, is convincingly and very attractively human, yet in others is, as we noted, a see-through mechanism, recalling the popular toys of the 1960s, the Visible Woman and the Visible Man; and that combination is especially arresting, because it repeatedly invites the eye to *different* assessments, blurring the conventional borders between thing and living being. Thus as Caleb talks to and increasingly becomes emotionally attached to Ava, he confesses that he finds her constantly "surprising"—perhaps a real instance of Bennett's "enchantment."

Moreover, Ava is a figure who puts the three robot paradigms we have discussed here into perspective, while also suggesting a possible direction for this figure's further cinematic development. Despite her seeming vulnerability, underscored by her highly feminine and physically slight appearance, as well as her plastic component parts, Ava, in fact, proves to be a powerful figure—much like any of the tin can figures discussed here or even Athena of *Tomorrowland*—demonstrating the force of the machine parts we can see working inside her. In her efforts to escape from her confinement and possible relegation to Nathan's closet of junked and forgotten prototypes, late in the narrative she manages to subdue Caleb and kill Nathan. Like Robby the Robot, she also has a mind of her own and, as Nathan offers, a much more advanced mind than most humans, although that mind seems little troubled by any Laws of Robotics. She rather easily convinces Caleb of her human-like capabilities, even genuine feelings for him, as she plots her escape from Nathan's maximum-security compound and tricks him into helping her. And after donning additional pieces of synthetic skin harvested from Nathan's other robot figures, some makeup, and a wig, she similarly

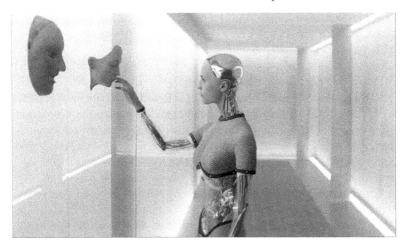

Figure 5.3 Ava (Alicia Vikander) inspects other possible "looks" or forms she might adopt in Alex Garland's *Ex Machina* (2015). Universal.

fools Nathan's helicopter pilot into taking her for human and flying her back to the city, where, as the final shot offers, she easily passes for human, blending right into the crowds of ordinary people. Looking quite human and with an advanced intelligence that has allowed her to outwit her male creator and male evaluator, Ava seems ready not only to determine her own future, but also to challenge conventional conceptions of what constitutes live-ness.

In this development, she also suggests a possible future for the skin job narrative, for other robot films that are sure to follow. Ava's demonstrated capabilities certainly present her as a kind of iconic representation of the power and emergence of women in contemporary culture, although that representative function of the skin job is hardly new or surprising. Among many others, films like *Eve of Destruction* (1991), *Steel and Lace* (1991), *Cherry 2000* (1988), the two versions of *The Stepford Wives* (1975, 2004), and television series such as *Battlestar Galactica* (2004–09), *Terminator: The Sarah Connor Chronicles* (2008–09), and *My Living Doll* (1964–65), have all traveled this same path, tapping into the robotic figure's ability to foreground how much of gender is quite literally constructed and thus to interrogate the formation of gender roles in contemporary culture. Ava's ability to manipulate or fashion her own image, however, adds a further dimension to such interrogations. And as contemporary culture, especially in the United States, becomes more diverse and more sensitive to issues of difference, we should only expect to see further uses of the skin job to metaphorize and explore the forceful emergence of variously marginalized groups, especially to examine how both difference and sameness can prove to be equally constructed categories. However, this figure also holds out the potential for more complex examinations, particularly those linked to what we earlier described as a posthuman "species."

In this context, we might briefly note Rosi Braidotti's claim for the potential impact of robotic bodies and synthetic intelligence on the very fabric of society, not just in terms of labor, but also in regard to ethical formulations. Extrapolating from the projected incorporation of artificial minds and figures into everyday life, she suggests that such technological developments will make it possible "to by-pass human decision making at both the operational and the moral levels," leaving humans not quite "out of the loop," but, as she offers, "on the loop," that is, monitoring—or so we might hope—our essentially autonomous machines as they go about their work and even make their own decisions on that work (44). This situation is, she argues, a pointedly "posthuman" one, because "it does not assume a human, individualized self" that will serve as the "deciding factor" in a particular circumstance, but rather a nexus of human, machine, and a "pre-defined" machinic "ethical system"—or what we might think of as a wholly new version of Asimov's Laws of Robotics—that will determine the best or most efficient patterns of action (45). This sort of scenario would forecast not so much the simple robots-run-amok situation that seems to arise in many earlier robot films, whether of the tin can, electronic wonder, or skin job meme, but rather narratives about robot–human partnerships, with a robotic "ethical system" set in measure against limited, exhausted, or corrupted human systems in determining a proper direction for "life," however we come to define that quality. In effect, this situation is what *Tomorrowland* offers us with Athena who has determined, *on her own* and despite Governor Nix's orders to cease her efforts, to recruit figures like Casey in order to "fix the future." Such narratives place the human in precisely the sort of "entangled" situation that Jane Bennett sees as the true underlying circumstance of life, the situation that, as contemporary humans, we often seem to want to disregard, to push beyond the boundaries of culture or consideration (*Vibrant* 115). Yet the new sort of skin job story might well afford us a different way of addressing the human relationship to the world in all of its "vibrant" character; it could open the door for our films to explore what Donna Haraway has influentially described as the ongoing "reinvention of nature."

However, the precise nature of that "reinvention" or the entanglement from which it proceeds is not the central focus here. Film scholars are finally little qualified to make such assessments, and this book was from the start conceived as an offshoot of film genre study, if of a slightly unconventional sort: one situated within a larger media/cultural context or the sort of complex communication environment we have described as a media ecology. As a consequence, it has always proceeded from the notion that it was exploring context, intersections between films, and between films and other cultural concepts, ideas, and activities that can provide a needed texture to an sf cinema and to its history. So although this study opens a door on issues involved in the possible evolution of humanity—on *posthuman* concerns—it does so mainly by way of trying to describe the environment in which our sf films operate today and a trajectory that seems to be emerging from that environment. The robot, although a product of science and engineering, an insistent figure of literature, film, and television, a conception of the human imagination that long predates modern Western culture, has simply been a most useful and intriguing marker of those various intersections that are constantly implicated in every product of our sf cinema.

Of course, the robotic *idea* is far older than any film; in fact, as J. David Bolter aptly observes, "there was perhaps never a moment in the ancient or modern history" of Western culture "when no one was pursuing the idea of making a human being by other than the ordinary reproductive means" (201)—or *imagining* the process and its outcomes in various ways. But that idea has taken very distinct forms and flourished in telling ways in our films, as well as our other visual media, telling an interesting and indeed useful story about the sf cinema. As we have several times suggested, the robot is an image close to the heart of cinema itself, to what, as we earlier noted, Balazs termed its "mighty visual anthropomorphism." And that image's persistence reminds us not only of how much film serves as a mirror of our sense of self, but also how it frames that portrait technologically, letting us consider how our entanglement with technology—whether gears and pulleys, computers and relays, or bioengineered components and implants—affects our sense of self and our relationship to our world.

The robot image is also a significant instrument for the mission of sf as a genre, especially its productive efforts at a "cognitive estrangement," that is, at enabling us to see anew and question the self and the world. Those different articulations of the robotic that we have discussed here, all of them variously anthropomorphic, prompt viewers to examine their conventional notions of the human, especially as the human and the technological become ever more intricately involved. And although we know that these images have been especially empowered by and reflective of our latest film technology—by the medium's ability not simply to capture a reality in the finest detail, but to construct, as sf itself has always sought to do, whatever reality we might imagine or *need*—that technological imaging has become increasingly powerful. We might briefly consider a film like *Avatar* (2009), which, thanks to its state-of-the-art digital imagery, effectively envisions how downloading a human consciousness into an alien hybrid body might change one's perceptions of the human, even lead to a rejection of the human in favor of that more appealing, and in this film's vision, more physically capable, Other. *Avatar*'s tremendous success—at the box office and in the popular imagination—has prompted the Walt Disney Company to invest approximately $500 million into creating a theme park area, "Pandora: The Land of Avatar" (due to open in 2017), where, with the help of films, sets, and various sorts of audioanimatronics—including, we might suspect, Disney's latest robot innovations, its "Living Character Initiative" figures[3]—visitors might in turn imagine themselves as Pandorans, as perhaps something other than human (Chmeilewski and Keegan). Enabled by the latest technology, that opening up and even inhabiting of the artificial body, glimpsed in a number of those earlier tin can robot films, may become a viable and perhaps even subversive experience readily available to any theme park visitor.

Friedrich Kittler, in his examinations of the connections between media and technology, has suggested that what he terms "the age of media (not just since Turing's game of imitation) renders indistinguishable what is human and what is machine" (146). It is a reminder not only of how film often blurs boundaries—always fashioning its own wondrous realities for our consumption and powerfully suggesting their substantiality—but also of how nearly allied film has always seemed to be to the work of sf. And that nearness, as I have tried to suggest here, is particularly underscored in the medium's robot work, as it seizes upon the latest digital technology to offer visions of the self that are indistinguishable from the real—as if the movies were, in fact, the ultimate manufacturer of robots. It is in this capacity that our visual media (and we should include here our theme parks, which are, after all, designed like movies) also replicate and confront us with the very issues that have always been bound up in human conceptions of the robotic being. The three key dimensions of this robot ecology have to date foregrounded and even linked these issues for our consideration: issues of power, issues of intelligent control, issues of self-meaning and self-determination. Empowered by the sf imagination, however, and as demonstrated by the Disney Living Character robotics, our media can and certainly seem ready to envision additional possibilities, potentially providing us with even more enchanting visions of the self in Tomorrowland.

Notes

1 Robert Romanyshyn in his *Technology as Symptom and Dream* has offered a more complex analysis of how the worldview attached to science and technology has produced "a distancing and detached vision" (117) similar to that which Bennett more recently describes—a vision that has also resulted in the

"body's broken connection to the world" (131–32), or what she would term "disenchantment."

2 The Turing Test, named after pioneering computer scientist Alan Turing, uses language interaction to determine if a machine might convincingly imitate human thought. It uses responses to a human's questions as a gauge of the machine's own human-like behavior. In the case of *Ex Machina*, of course, several of the primary components of such a test, such as the withholding of actual speech or of the appearance of the machine, have been removed from the equation, effectively shifting the element of human imitation to emotional or logical manipulations.

3 The Disney Living Character Initiative has, to date, produced a variety of seemingly independent robotic characters, such as Lucky the Dinosaur, the Muppet Mobile Lab, and the Amazing Destini. Earlier versions of these audio-animatronic figures were essentially robotic puppets, electronically controlled at a distance by an unseen puppeteer. The most recent efforts, though, such as the Amazing Destini, function independently. As Disney Imagineer Josh Gorin explains, "There is no live human operator involved"; it is just a robotic character "using sophisticated computers, sensors, and artificial intelligence to understand what guests are saying and doing and respond in character" to them (quoted in Leibacher).

A Select Filmography/Videography

The following is a listing of various films, serials, and television series that centrally feature robots, androids, or cyborgs or that are often cited in discussions of such figures. It is not an exhaustive list. For additional titles, see the filmography in my *Replications: A Robotic History of the Science Fiction Film* and the videography attached to my *The Essential Science Fiction Television Reader*.

A.I. Artificial Intelligence (2001). Amblin Entertainment/Stanley Kubrick Productions/Warner Bros. Dir.: Steven Spielberg. Script: Steven Spielberg. Cast: Haley Joel Osment, Jude Law, William Hurt, Frances O'Connor.

Alien (1979). 20th Century Fox. Prod.: Gordon Carroll. Dir.: Ridley Scott. Script: Dan O'Bannon. Cast: Tom Skerritt, Sigourney Weaver, Ian Holm.

Aliens (1986). 20th Century Fox. Prod.: Gale Ann Hurd. Dir.: James Cameron. Script: Cameron. Cast: Sigourney Weaver, Michael Biehn, Lance Henriksen.

Alien 3 (1992). Brandywine/20th Century Fox. Dir.: David Fincher. Script: David Giler, Walter Hill, Larry Ferguson. Cast: Sigourney Weaver, Charles Dance, Charles S. Dutton.

Alien: Resurrection (1997). Brandywine/20th Century Fox. Dir.: Jean-Pierre Jeunet. Script: Joss Whedon. Cast: Sigourney Weaver, Winona Ryder, Ron Perlman.

Almost Human (2013–14). Bad Robot Productions/Warner Bros. TV/Fox. Created by J. H. Wyman. Dir.: Brad Anderson, Sam Hill, et al. Script: J. H. Wyman, Alison Schapker, et al. Cast: Karl Urban, Michael Ealy, Minka Kelly, Lili Taylor.

American Cyborg (1994). Cannon Pictures. Dir.: Boaz Davidson. Script: Brent Friedman, Bill Crounse, Don Pequignot. Cast: Joe Lara, Nicole Hansen, John Ryan.

Android (1982). Island Alive/New World. Dir.: Aaron Lipstadt. Script: James Reigle, Don Opper. Cast: Klaus Kinski, Norbert Weisser, Don Opper.

Avatar (2009). Lightstorm/Dune/20th Century Fox. Dir.: James Cameron. Script: James Cameron. Cast: Sam Worthington, Zoe Saldana, Stephen Lang, Sigourney Weaver.

Battlestar Gallactica (1978–80). Glen A. Larson Productions/MCA/ABC. Created by Glen A. Larson. Dir.: Rod Holcomb, Christian Nyby II, Daniel Haller, et al. Script: Glen A. Larson, Donald P. Bellisario, Michael Sloan, et al. Cast: Richard Hatch, Lorne Greene, Dirk Benedict, Maren Jensen.

Battlestar Galactica (2004–09). British Sky Broadcasting/David Eick Productions/ SyFy Channel. Dir.: Michael Rhymer, Rod Hardy, Edward James Olmos, et al. Script: Ronald D. Moore, David Eick, Toni Graphia, et al. Cast: Edward James Olmos, Mary McDonnell, Katee Sackhoff, James Callis. Based on the earlier Glen A. Larson series.

Big Hero 6 (2014). Walt Disney Pictures. Dir.: Don Hall, Chris Williams. Script: Jordan Roberts, Dan Gerson, Robert L. Baird. Voice Actors: Ryan Potter, Scott Adsit, Daniel Henney, T. J. Miller, Damon Wayans, Jr. Animated.

The Bionic Woman (1976–78). Harve Bennett Productions/Universal TV/ABC/ NBC. Created by Kenneth Johnson. Dir.: Alan Crosland, Alan J. Levi, et al. Script: Kenneth Johnson, James D. Parriott, et al. Cast: Lindsay Wagner, Richard Anderson, Christopher Stone.

The Black Hole (1979). Walt Disney Productions. Dir.: Gary Nelson. Script: Jeb Rosebrook, Gerry Day. Cast: Maximilian Schell, Robert Forster, Yvette Mimieux.

Blade Runner (1982). Warner Bros. Producer: Michael Deeley. Director: Ridley Scott. Script: Hampton Fancher, David Peoples. Cast: Harrison Ford, Rutger Hauer, Sean Young.

Buck Rogers in the 25th Century (1979–81). John Mantley Productions/Glen A. Larson Productions/Universal TV/NBC. Created by Glen A. Larson and Leslie Stevens. Dir.: Daniel Haller, Dick Lowry, et al. Script: Larson, Stevens, Alan Brennert, Anne Collins, et al. Cast: Gil Gerard, Erin Gray, Felix Silla.

Captain Video: Master of the Stratosphere (1951). Columbia. Dir.: Spencer Gordon Bennet, Wallace Grissell. Script: Sherman L. Lowe, Joseph F. Poland, Royal K. Cole. Cast: Judd Holdren, George Eldredge, Gene Roth. Serial in 15 chapters.

Chappie (2015). Media Rights/Columbia Pictures. Dir.: Neill Blomkamp. Script: Neill Blomkamp, Terri Tatchell. Cast: Sharlto Copley, Dev Patel, Yolandi Visser.

Cherry 2000 (1987). Orion Pictures. Dir.: Steve De Jarnatt. Script: Michael Almereyda. Cast: Melanie Griffith, David Andrews, Tim Thomerson.

Circuitry Man (1990). IRS Media/Skouras Films. Dir.: Steven Lovy. Script: Steven and Robert Lovy. Cast: Jim Metzler, Dana Wheeler-Nicholson, Vernon Wells.

A Clever Dummy (1917). Keystone/Triangle. Dir.: Herman C. Raymaker, Ferris Hartman, Robert Kerr. Script: Mack Sennett. Cast: Ben Turpin, Chester Conklin, Wallace Beery.

The Colossus of New York (1958). Paramount. Dir.: Eugene Lourie. Script: Thelma Schnee. Cast: Ross Martin, Mala Powers, Otto Kruger.

Commando Cody: Sky Marshal of the Universe (1953). Republic. Dir.: Harry Keller, Franklin Adreon, Fred C. Brannon. Script: Ronald Davidson, Barry Shipman. Cast: Judd Holdren, Aline Towne, Gregory Gaye. Serial in 12 chapters.

Creature from the Black Lagoon (1954). Universal. Dir.: Jack Arnold. Script: Harry Essex, Arthur A. Ross. Cast: Richard Carlson, Julia Adams, Richard Denning.

Cyborg (1989). Canon. Dir.: Albert Pyun. Script: Kitty Chalmers. Cast: Jean-Claude Van Damme, Deborah Richter, Vincent Klyn, Alex Daniels.

Cyborg 2087 (1966). United Pictures/Republic. Dir.: Franklin Adreon. Script: Arthur C. Pierce. Cast: Michael Rennie, Karen Steele, Wendell Corey, Warren Stevens.

Dancing Lady (1933). MGM. Dir.: Robert Z. Leonard. Script: Allen Rivkin, P. J. Wolfson. Cast: Clark Gable, Joan Crawford, Franchot Tone.

D.A.R.Y.L. (1985). Paramount. Dir.: Simon Wincer. Script: David Ambrose, Allan Scott, Jeffrey Ellis. Cast: Barret Oliver, Mary Beth Hurt, Michael McKean.

The Day the Earth Stood Still (1951). 20th Century Fox. Dir.: Robert Wise. Script: Edmund North. Cast: Michael Rennie, Patricia Neal, Sam Jaffe.

Demon Seed (1977). MGM. Dir.: Donald Cammell. Script: Robert Jaffe, Roger O. Hirson. Cast: Julie Christie, Fritz Weaver, Gerrit Graham.

Devil Girl from Mars (1954). Danziger/Spartan. Dir.: David MacDonald. Script: James Eastwood. Cast: Patricia Laffan, Hugh McDermott, Hazel Court.

Doctor Who (1963–89, 1996, 2005-present). BBC/BBC Wales/Canadian Broadcasting Corp. Dir.: Russell T. Davies, Steven Moffat, et al. Script: Davies, Moffat, Robert Holmes, Douglas Adams, et al. Cast: Tom Baker, David Tennant, Matt Smith, Peter Capaldi, et al.

Dollhouse (2009–10). Mutant Enemy Productions/20th Century Fox. Dir.: Joss Whedon, Tim Minear, David Solomon. Script: Joss Whedon, Jed Whedon, Tim Minear, et al. Cast: Eliza Dushku, Olivia Williams, Fran Kranz, Tahmoh Penikett.

The Empire Strikes Back (1980). Lucasfilm/20th Century Fox. Dir.: Irvin Kershner. Script: Leigh Brackett, Lawrence Kasdan. Cast: Mark Hamill, Harrison Ford, Carrie Fisher, Billy Dee Williams.

Eve of Destruction (1991). Interscope Communications/Nelson Ent./Orion. Dir.: Duncan Gibbins, Scripit: Gibbins, Yale Udoff. Cast: Renee Soutendjik, Gregory Hines.

Ex Machina (2015). DNA Films/Film4/Scott Rudin Prods. Dir.: Alex Garland. Script: Garland. Cast: Domhnall Gleeson, Alicia Vikander, Oscar Isaac.

Firefly (2001–02). 20th Century Fox/Syfy Channel. Created by Joss Whedon. Dir.: Joss Whedon, Tim Minear, et al. Script: Whedon, Minear, Jane Espenson, et al. Cast: Nathan Fillion, Summer Glau, Gina Torres, Alan Tudyk.

Flash Gordon (1936). Universal. Dir.: Frederick Stephani, Ray Taylor. Script: Stephani, George Plympton, Basil Dickey, Ella O'Neill. Cast: Larry "Buster" Crabbe, Jean Rogers, Charles Middleton, Frank Shannon. Serial in 13 chapters.

Forbidden Planet (1956). MGM. Dir.: Fred McLeod Wilcox. Script: Cyril Hume. Cast: Walter Pidgeon, Leslie Nielsen, Anne Francis.

Frankenstein (1931). Universal. Dir.: James Whale. Script: Garrett Fort, Francis Edward Farough. Cast: Boris Karloff, Colin Clive, Mae Clark.

Futurama (1999–2003, 2008–13). Curiosity Company/20th Century Fox/Fox. Created by Matt Groening. Dir.: Rich Moore, Peter Avanzino, et al. Script: Groening, David X. Cohen, Eric Horsted, et al. Voice Actors: Billy West, Katey Sagal, John DiMaddio, Lauren Tom. Animated series.

Futureworld (1976). American International. Dir.: Richard T. Heffron. Script: Mayo Simon, George Schenck. Cast: Peter Fonda, Blythe Danner, Arthur Hill, Yul Brynner.

Galaxina (1980). Crown International. Dir.: William Sachs. Script: William Sachs. Cast: Dorothy Stratten, Avery Schreiber, Stephen Macht.

Ghost in the Shell (1995). Bandai/Kodansha. Dir.: Mamoru Oshii. Script: Kazunori Ito. Voice Actors: Atsuko Tanaka, Akio Otsuka, Koichi Yamadera. Animated.

Gog (1954). Ivan Tors Productions/United Artists. Dir.: Herbert L. Strock. Script: Tom Taggart, Richard G. Taylor. Cast: Richard Egan, Constance Dowling, Herbert Marshall.

Gremlins (1984). Amblin Entertainment/Warner Bros. Dir.: Joe Dante. Script: Chris Columbus. Cast: Zach Galligan, Phoebe Cates, Hoyt Axton, Polly Holliday.

Hardware (1990). British Satellite Broadcasting/Millimeter Films. Dir.: Richard Stanley. Script: Richard Stanley. Cast: Dylan McDermott, Stacey Travis, John Lynch.

Heartbeeps (1981). Universal. Dir.: Allan Arkush. Script: John Hill. Cast: Andy Kaufman, Bernadette Peters, Randy Quaid.

The Human Duplicators (1965). Allied Artists. Dir.: Hugo Grimaldi. Script: Arthur C. Pierce. Cast: George Nader, Barbara Nichols, George Macready.

I, Robot (2004). Davis Entertainment/Overbrook Films/20th Century Fox. Dir.: Alex Proyas. Script: Jeff Vintar, Akiva Goldsman. Cast: Will Smith, Bridget Moynahan, Bruce Greenwood.

The Inventor's Secret (1911). Biograph Company. Dir.: Mack Sennett. Script: George Hennessy. Cast: Mack Sennett, Mabel Normand, Ford Sterling.

The Invisible Boy (1957). MGM. Dir.: Herman Hoffman. Script: Cyril Hume, Edmund Cooper. Cast: Richard Eyer, Philip Abbott, Diane Brewster, Harold J. Stone.

The Iron Giant (1999). Warner Bros. Dir.: Brad Bird. Script: Tim McCanilies. Voice Actors: Eli Marienthal, Christopher McDonald, Jennifer Aniston, Harry Connick, Jr. Animated.

The Jetsons (1962–63, 1985–87). Screen Gems/World Vision Enterprises/Warner Bros./ABC. Created by Hanna-Barbera Productions. Dir.: William Hanna, Joseph Barbera, et al. Script: Hanna, Barbera, et al. Voice Actors: George O'Hanlon, Penny Singleton, Daws Butler, Mel Blanc. Animated series.

Kronos (1957). Regal Films/20th Century Fox. Dir.: Kurt Neumann. Script: Lawrence Louis Goldman. Cast: Jeff Morrow, Barbara Lawrence, John Emery, Morris Ankrum.

Leave It to Roll-Oh (1940). Jam Handy Organization/Chevrolet/General Motors. Advertising film from 1939–40 New York World's Fair.

Lost in Space (1965–68). 20th Century Fox/Irwin Allen Productions/CBS. Dir.: Irwin Allen, Harry Harris, Nathan H. Juran, et al. Script: Allen, Norman Lessing, et al. Cast: Guy Williams, June Lockhart, Billy Mumy, Jonathan Harris.

Lost in Space (1998). Jim Henson's Creature Shop/New Line Cinema. Dir.: Stephen Hopkins. Script: Akiva Goldsman. Cast: Gary Oldman, William Hurt, Matt Le Blanc, Heather Graham.

Making Mr. Right (1987). Orion. Dir.: Susan Seidelman. Script: Floyd Byars, Laurie Frank. Cast: John Malkovic, Ann Magnuson, Glenne Headley.

Mann & Machine (1992). Universal TV/Wolf Films/NBC. Created by Robert De Laurentiis, Dick Wolf. Cast: David Andrews, Yancy Butler, S. Epatha Merkerson.

Master of the World (*Der Herr der Welt*, 1934). Ariel Film-Verleih. Dir.: Harry Piel. Script: Georg Muhlen-Schulte. Cast: Walter Janssen, Sybille Schmitz, Aribert Wascher, Siegfried Schurenberg.

The Master Mystery (1919). Octagon Films/Pathe. Dir.: Burton L. King, Harry Grossman. Script: Arthur B. Reeve, Charles Logue. Cast: Harry Houdini, Marguerite Marsh, Ruth Stonehouse.

The Mechanical Man (1921). Milano Film. Dir.: Andre Deed. Script: Deed. Cast: Deed, Valentina Frascaroli, Mathilde Lambert, Giulia Costa.

Metropolis (1927). UFA. Dir.: Fritz Lang. Script: Thea von Harbou, Lang. Cast: Alfred Abel, Brigitte Helm, Gustav Froelich, Rudolph Klein-Rogge.

Metropolis (2001). Madhouse/Toho. Dir.: Rintaro. Script: Katsuhiro Otomo. Voice Actors: Kei Kobayashi, Yuka Imoto, Taro Ishida, Kosei Tomita. Animated.

The Monster and the Ape (1945). Columbia. Dir.: Howard Bretherton. Script: Royal K. Cole, Sherman L. Lowe. Cast: Robert Lowery, George Macready, Ralph Morgan, Carole Matthews. Serial in 15 chapters.

My Living Doll (1964–65). Jack Chertok Productions/CBS. Dir.: Lawrence Dobkin, Ezra Stone. Script: Bill Kelsay, Al Martin, Bernard Slade, et al. Cast: Bob Cummings, Julie Newmar, Jack Mullaney.

The Mysterians (1957). Toho Co./MGM. Dir.: Ishiro Honda. Script: Shigeru Kayama, Takeshi Kimura. Cast: Kenji Sahara, Yumi Shirakawa, Momoko Kochi, Takashi Shimura.

Mysterious Doctor Satan (1940). Republic. Dir.: William Whitney, John English. Script: Franklyn Adreon, Ronald Davidson, Norman S. Hall, Joseph F. Poland, Barney A. Sarecky, Sol Shor. Cast: Eduardo Ciannelli, Robert Wilcox, William Newell. Serial in 15 chapters.

The Outer Limits (1963–65, 1995–2002). Villa Di Stefano/Daystar Productions/ MGM/ABC. Created by Leslie Stevens. Dir.: John Brahm, Abner Biberman, Byron Haskin, et al. Script: Leslie Stevens, Joseph Stefano, Harlan Ellison, et al. Cast: Vic Perrin (Control Voice/Narrator).

The Perfect Woman (1949). Two Cities/General Film Distributors-UK. Dir.: Bernard Knowles. Script: George Black, Bernard Knowles. Cast: Patricia Roc, Stanley Holloway, Nigel Patrick.

The Phantom Creeps (1939). Universal. Dir.: Ford Beebe, Saul A. Goodkind. Script: Mildred Barish, Willis Cooper, Basil Dickey, George Plymptom. Cast: Bela Lugosi, Robert Kent, Dorothy Arnold. Serial in 12 chapters.

The Phantom Empire (1935). Mascot. Dir.: Otto Brower, B. Reeves Eason. Script: Wallace MacDonald, Gerald Geraghty, H. Freedman. Cast: Gene Autry, Smiley Burnette, Frankie Darro, Betsy Ross King. Serial in 12 chapters.

Planet of Storms (*Planeta Bur*, 1962). Lennauchfilm, USSR. Dir.: Pavel Klushantsev. Script: Aleksandr Kazantsev, Pavel Klushantsev. Cast: Vladimir Yemelyanov, Georgiy Zhzhonov, Yuri Sarantsev.

Prometheus (2012). Scott Free/Brandywine/Dune Entertainment/20th Century Fox. Dir.: Ridley Scott. Script: Jon Spaihts, Damon Lindelof. Cast: Noomi Rapace, Michael Fassbender, Guy Pearce, Charlize Theron.

Radar Men from the Moon (1951). Republic. Dir.: Fred C. Brannon. Script: Ronald Davidson. Cast: George Wallace, Roy Barcroft, Clayton Moore. Serial in 12 chapters.

Red Dwarf (1988–93, 1997–99, 2009, 2012–13). BBC/Grant Naylor Productions/ Paul Jackson Productions/BBC2. Created by Rob Grant and Doug Naylor. Cast: Craig Charles, Danny John-Jules, Chris Barrie, Robert Llewellyn.

Return of the Jedi (1983). Lucasfilm/20th Century Fox. Dir.: Richard Marquand. Script: Lawrence Kasdan, George Lucas. Cast: Mark Hamill, Harrison Ford, Carrie Fisher, Billy Dee Williams.

Revenge of the Stepford Wives (1980). Embassy. Dir.: Robert Fuest. Script: David Wiltse. Cast: Sharon Gless, Julie Kavner, Don Johnson, Arthur Hill.

RoboCop (1987). Orion. Dir.: Paul Verhoeven. Script: Edward Neumeier, Arne Schmidt. Cast: Peter Weller, Nancy Allen, Ronny Cox.

RoboCop 2 (1990). Orion. Dir.: Irvin Kershner. Script: Frank Miller, Walon Green. Cast: Peter Weller, Nancy Allen, Daniel O'Herlihy.

Robocop 3 (1993). Orion. Dir.: Fred Dekker. Script: Dekker, Frank Miller. Cast: Robert John Burke, Nancy Allen, Rip Torn.

Robocop: The Series (1994). Robocop Productions/Rysher Entertainment/Skyvision Entertainment. Producer and Created by: Stephen Downing. Cast: Richard Eden, Yvette Nipar, Andrea Roth.

Robot Carnival (1987). Studio APPP/Streamline Pictures. Dir.: Atsuko Fukushima, Katsuhiro Otomo, et al. Script: Otomo, Hiroyuki Kitakubo, et al. Voice Actors: Koji Moritsugu, Yayoi Maki, Keiko Hanagata. Animated.

Robot Monster (1953). Astor Pictures. Dir.: Phil Tucker. Script: Wyott Ordung. Cast: George Nader, Claudia Barrett, Selena Royale.

Robot Overlords (2014). Embankment/Vertical Entertainment. Dir.: Jon Wright. Script: Wright, Mark Stay. Cast: Callan McAuliffe, Ben Kingsley, Gillian Anderson.

Robots (2005). Blue Sky/20th Century Fox. Dir. Chris Wedge. Script: David Lindsay- Abaire, Lowell Ganz, Babaloo Mandel. Voice Actors: Ewan McGregor, Halle Berry, Greg Kinnear, Mel Brooks. Animated.

Runaway (1984). TriStar Pictures. Dir.: Michael Crichton. Script: Crichton. Cast: Tom Selleck, Cynthia Rhodes, Gene Simmons, Kirstie Alley.

Saturn 3 (1980). ITC Entertainment. Dir.: Stanley Donen. Script: Martin Amis. Cast: Kirk Douglas, Farrah Fawcett, Harvey Keitel.

Serenity (2005). Universal. Dir.: Joss Whedon. Script: Whedon. Cast: Nathan Fillion, Gina Torres, Summer Glau, Alan Tudyk.

Short Circuit (1986). PSO/Tristar. Dir.: John Badham. Script: S. S. Wilson, Brent Maddock. Cast: Steven Guttenberg, Ally Sheedy, Fisher Stevens.

Silent Running (1972). Michael Gruskoff Prods./Universal. Dir.: Douglas Trumbull. Script: Deric Washburn, Michael Cimino, Steve Bochco. Cast: Bruce Dern, Cliff Potts, Ron Rifkin.

Silent Star (*First Spaceship on Venus*, *Der Schweigende Stern*, 1960). VEB-DEFA-Studio fur Spielfilme, East German-Polish co-production. Dir.: Kurt Maetzig. Script: Maetzig, J. Barkhauer. Cast: Gunther Simon, Yoko Tani, Julius Ongewe, Kurt Rackelmann.

The Six Million Dollar Man (1974–78). Harve Bennett Productions/Universal/ ABC. Dir.: Russ Mayberry, Richard Irving, et al. Script: Glen A. Larson, Elroy Schwartz, et al. Cast: Lee Majors, Richard Anderson, Martin E. Brooks, Farrah Fawcett.

Sky Captain and the World of Tomorrow (2004). Filmauro/Brooklyn Films/Paramount. Dir.: Kerry Conran. Script: Kerry Konran. Cast: Jude Law, Gwyneth Paltrow, Angelina Jolie.

Sleeper (1973). Rollins-Joffe/United Artists. Dir.: Woody Allen. Script: Allen, Marshall Brickman. Cast: Woody Allen, Diane Keaton, John Beck.

Star Trek: First Contact (1996). Paramount. Dir.: Jonathan Frakes. Script: Brannon Braga, Ronald D. Moore. Cast: Patrick Stewart, Jonathan Frakes, Brent Spiner, Gates McFadden.

Star Trek: The Next Generation (1987–94). Paramount TV/CBS. Spin-off of *Star Trek*. Creator and Executive Producer: Gene Roddenberry. Cast: Patrick Stewart, Jonathan Frakes, LeVar Burton, Brent Spiner, Marina Sirtis.

Star Wars (aka *A New Hope*, 1977). 20th Century Fox. Dir.: George Lucas. Script: Lucas. Cast: Mark Hamill, Harrison Ford, Carrie Fisher, Alec Guiness.

Star Wars: The Clone Wars (2008–13). CGCG Inc./Lucasfilm/Cartoon Network. Dir.: Dave Filoni. Script: Katie Lucas, Drew Greenberg, Steven Melching, George Lucas, Cameron Litvack, Dave Filoni. Voice Actors: Matt Lanter, Ashley Eckstein, James Arnold Taylor, Tom Kane. Animated series.

Star Wars: Episode 1—The Phantom Menace (1999). Lucasfilm/20th Century Fox. Dir.: George Lucas. Script: Lucas. Cast: Liam Neeson, Ewan McGregor, Natalie Portman, Jake Lloyd.

The Stepford Wives (1975). Fadsin Cinema Assoc./Paloma/Columbia. Dir.: Bryan Forbes. Script: William Goldman. Cast: Katherine Ross, Paula Prentiss, Peter Masterson, Tina Louise.

The Stepford Wives (2004). Paramount/Dreamworks. Dir.: Frank Oz. Script: Paul Rudnick. Cast: Nicole Kidman, Matthew Broderick, Bette Midler.

Target Earth (1954). Allied Artists. Dir.: Sherman A. Rose. Script: William Raynor. Cast: Richard Denning, Kathleen Crowley, Virginia Gray, Dick Reeves.

The Terminator (1984). Helmdale Film/Orion Pictures. Dir.: James Cameron. Script: Cameron, Gale Anne Hurd, William Wisher, Jr. Cast: Arnold Schwarzenegger, Linda Hamilton, Michael Biehn.

Terminator 2: Judgment Day (1991). Carolco Pictures/TriStar Pictures. Dir.: James Cameron. Script: Cameron, William Wisher, Jr. Cast: Arnold Schwarzenegger, Linda Hamilton, Edward Furlong, Robert Patrick.

Terminator 3: Rise of the Machines (2003). IMF/C2 Pictures/Warner Bros. Dir.: Jonathan Mostow. Script: John Brancato, Michael Ferris. Cast: Arnold Schwarzenegger, Nick Stahl, Claire Danes, Kristanna Loken.

Terminator Genisys (2015). Skydance/Paramount. Dir.: Alan Taylor. Script: Laeta Kalogridis, Patrick Lussier. Cast: Arnold Schwarzenegger, Jason Clarke, Emilia Clarke, Matt Smith.

Terminator Salvation (2009). Halcyon/Wonderland/Warner Bros. Dir.: McG. Script: John Brancato, Michael Ferris. Cast: Christian Bale, Sam Worthington, Anton Yelchin.

Terminator: The Sarah Connor Chronicles (2008–09). C2 Pictures/Warner Bros./ Fox. Creator: Josh Friedman. Dir.: David Nutter, Paul Edwards, et al. Script: John Friedman, John Wirth, et al. Cast: Lena Headey, Thomas Dekker, Summer Glau. Based on the *Terminator* film series.

THX 1138 (1971). Warner Bros. Dir.: George Lucas. Script: Lucas, Walter Murch. Cast: Robert Duvall, Donald Pleasence, Maggie McOmie.

Tobor the Great (1954). Republic. Dir.: Lee Sholem. Script: Carl Dudley, Philip MacDonald. Cast: Charles Drake, Karin Booth, Billy Chapin.

Tomorrowland (2015). Walt Disney Pictures. Dir.: Brad Bird. Script: Bird, Damon Lindelof, Jeff Jensen. Cast: George Clooney, Britt Robertson, Hugh Laurie, Raffey Cassidy.

Tron (1982). Lisberger/Kuchner/Walt Disney Prods. Dir.: Steven Lisberger. Script: Lisberger. Cast: Jeff Bridges, David Warner, Bruce Boxleitner, Cindy Morgan.

Tron: Legacy (2010). Walt Disney Pictures. Dir.: Joseph Kosinski. Script: Edward Kitsis, Adam Horowitz. Cast: Jeff Bridges, Garrett Hedlund, Olivia Wilde, Bruce Boxleitner.

Tron: Uprising (2012–13). Disney/ABC/Disney XD. Dir.: Charlie Bean. Developed by Edward Kitsis, Adam Horowitz. Voice Actors: Elijah Wood, Bruce Boxleitner, Mandy Moore, Nate Corddry. Animated series.

The Twilight Zone (1959–64). Cayuga Productions/CBS. Creator/Writer/Producer: Rod Serling. Directors: John Brahm, Mitch Leisen, Jacques Tourneur, et al. Script: Serling, Charles Beaumont, Richard Matheson, et al. Cast: Rod Serling (narrator).

Undersea Kingdom (1936). Republic. Dir.: Joseph Kane, B. Reeves Eason. Script: John Rathmell, Maurice Geraghty, Oliver Drake. Cast: Ray "Crash" Corrigan, Monte Blue, William Farnum, Lon Chaney, Jr. Serial in 12 chapters.

The Vanishing Shadow (1934). Universal. Dir.: Lew Landers. Script: Basil Dickey, George Morgan, Ella O'Neil, Het Mannheim. Cast: Onslow Stevens, Ada Ince, James Durkin. Serial in 12 chapters.

WALL-E (2008). Walt Disney Pictures/Pixar. Dir.: Andrew Stanton. Script: Stanton, Jim Reardon. Voice Actors: Ben Burtt, Elissa Knight, Fred Willard, John Ratzenberger. Animated.

Westworld (1973). MGM. Dir.: Michael Crichton. Script: Crichton. Cast: Richard Benjamin, James Brolin, Yul Brynner.

Zombies of the Stratosphere (aka *Satan's Satellites*, (1952). Republic. Dir.: Fred C. Brannon. Script: Ronald Davidson. Cast: Judd Holdren, Aline Towne, Wilson Wood, Lane Bradford. Serial in 12 chapters.

A Selective Bibliography

The following listing includes all works cited in this volume, as well as others that have been useful in pursuing and formulating its ideas.

Adkins, Richard. E-mail to the Author. 18 August 2014.

Ahmed, Rida. "Japan Unveils World's First Eerily Human Robot Newscaster with a Sense of Humor." *HNGN* June 24, 2014. www.hngn.com/articles/34479/20140624/ Japan-unveils-world-s-first-eerilly-human-robot-newscaster-sense.htm. Accessed Sept. 18, 2014. Web.

Altman, Rick. "A Semantic/Syntactic Approach to Film Genre." *Film Theory and Criticism*. 6th ed. Eds. Leo Braudy and Marshall Cohen. New York: Oxford UP, 2004. 680–90.

Asimov, Isaac. *I, Robot*. Greenwich, CT: Fawcett-Crest, 1950.

Balazs, Bela. *Theory of the Film: Character and Growth of a New Art*. Trans. Edith Bone. New York: Dover, 1970.

Barton, Fred. "Robby the Robot." www.the-robotman.com. Accessed June 24, 2014. Web.

Bennett, Jane. *The Enchantment of Modern Life: Attachments, Crossing, and Ethics*. Princeton: Princeton UP, 2001.

———.*Vibrant Matter: A Political Ecology of Things*. Durham: Duke UP, 2010.

Blackmore, Susan. *The Meme Machine*. Oxford: Oxford UP, 1999.

Bergson, Henri. "Laughter." 1900. Trans. Cloudesley Brereton and Fred Rothwell. *The Comic in Theory and Practice*. Ed. John J. Enck, Elizabeth T. Forter, and Alvin Whitley. New York: Appleton-Century, 1960. 43–64.

Bolter, J. David. *Turing's Man: Western Culture in the Computer Age*. Chapel Hill: U of North Carolina P, 1984.

Braidotti, Rosi. *The Posthuman*. London: Polity Press, 2013.

Capek, Karel. *R. U. R.* Trans. Paul Selver. Oxford: Oxford UP, 1961.

Casetti, Francesco. *Eye of the Century: Film, Experience, and Modernity*. Trans. Erin Larkin with Jennifer Pranolo. New York: Columbia UP, 2005.

Chapman, James, and Nicholas J. Cull. *Projecting Tomorrow: Science Fiction and Popular Cinema*. London: I. B. Tauris, 2013.

Chmielewski, Dawn C., and Rebecca Keegan. "Disney to License Rights to 'Avatar' for Theme Park Attractions." *Los Angeles Times* Sept. 21, 2011.

www.articles.latimes.com/2011/set/21/business/la-fi-ct-disney-avatar-2011092. Accessed June 21, 2015. Web.

Clarke, Frederick S, and Steve Rubin. "Making Forbidden Planet." *Cinefantastique* 8.2–3 (1979): 4–66.

"A Clever Mechanical and Electrical Automaton." *Scientific American* 94.2 (1906): 46.

Cline, William C. *In the Nick of Time: Motion Picture Sound Serials.* Jefferson, NC: McFarland, 1984.

Cohen, John. *Human Robots in Myth and Science.* Cranbury, NJ: Barnes, 1967.

Crowther, Bosley. "'Forbidden Planet' Is Out of This World." *The New York Times.* May 4, 1956. www.nytimes.com/movie/review. Accessed April 10, 2014. Web.

Dawkins, Richard. *The Selfish Gene: 30th Anniversary Edition.* Oxford: Oxford UP, 2006.

Fuller, Matthew. *Media Ecologies: Materialist Energies in Art and Technoculture.* Cambridge: MIT Press, 2005.

Fulton, Roger. *The Encyclopedia of TV Science Fiction.* 3rd ed. London: Boxtree, 1997.

Gallardo C., Ximena, and C. Jason Smith. *Alien Woman: The Making of Lt. Ellen Ripley.* New York: Continuum, 2004.

Geduld, Harry M., and Ronald Gottesman, eds. *Robots, Robots, Robots.* Boston: New York Graphic Society, 1978.

George, Susan. "Fraking Machines: Desire, Gender, and the (Post)Human Condition in *Battlestar Galactica.*" *The Essential Science Fiction Television Reader.* Ed. J. P. Telotte. Lexington: UP of Kentucky, 2008. 159–75.

Gunning, Tom, "The Cinema of Attraction: Early Film, Its Spectator and the Avant-Garde," Wide Angle 8. 3–4 (1986): 63–70.

Hall, Mordaunt. "*Dancing Lady.*" *The New York Times* Dec. 1, 1933. www.nytimes.com/movie/review. Accessed October 24, 2013.

Haraway, Donna. *Simians, Cyborgs, and Women: The Reinvention of Nature.* New York: Routledge, 1991.

Hill, Rodney. "Anthology Drama: Mapping *The Twilight Zone*'s Cultural and Mythological Terrain." *The Essential Science Fiction Television Reader.* Ed. J. P. Telotte. Lexington: UP of Kentucky, 2008. 111–26.

Hoggett, Reuben. "Pseudo Automata, Fakes and Robot Costumes." www.cyberneticzoo.com/pseudo-automata-fakes-robot-costumes. Accessed July 7, 2015. Web.

James, Edward. *Science Fiction in the Twentieth Century.* New York: Oxford UP, 1994.

Jenkins, Henry. *Convergence Culture: Where Old and New Media Collide.* New York: NYU Press, 2006.

———, Sam Ford, and Joshua Green. *Spreadable Media: Creating Value and Meaning in a Networked Culture.* New York: NYU Press, 2013.

Jones, Gwyneth. "The Icons of Science Fiction." *The Cambridge Companion to Science Fiction.* Eds. Edward James and Farah Mendlesohn. Cambridge: Cambridge UP, 2003. 163–73.

Kelly, Kevin. "Terminator, the Queen Borg in the Shell Chronicles." *Io9* Jan. 7, 2008. www.io9.com/341381/terminator-the-queen-borg-in-the-shell-chronicles. Accessed Sept. 9, 2014.

Kitahara, Teruhisa. *Robots: Tin Toy Dreams*. San Francisco: Chronicle Books, 1985.

Kittler, Friedrich A. *Gramophone, Film, Typewriter*. Trans. Geoffrey Winthrop-Young and Michael Wutz. Stanford: Stanford UP, 1999.

Krasnoff, Barbara. *Robots: Reel to Real*. New York: Arco, 1982.

Kuhn, Annette. "Introduction." *Alien Zone: Cultural Theory and Contemporary Science Fiction Cinema*. Ed. Annette Kuhn. London: Verso, 1990. 1–12.

Kurzweil, Ray. *The Age of Spiritual Machines: When Computers Exceed Human Intelligence*. New York: Penguin, 2000.

Landon, Brooks. *Science Fiction after 1900: From the Steam Man to the Stars*. New York: Routledge, 2002.

Leibacher, Herb. "Disney's Amazing Destini—The Future of Audio Animatronics?" *World of Walt*. www.worldofwalt.com/disney-destini.html. Accessed June 22, 2015. Web.

May, Bob. "An Interview with Actor Bob May." *The B9 Robot Builders Club*. http://www.b9robotbuildersclub.com/pub/home/may.html. Accessed Feb. 13, 2014. Web.

Miller, Cynthia J. "Defending the Heartland: Technology and the Future in *The Phantom Empire* (1935)." *Heroes of Film, Comics and American Culture: Essays on Real and Fictional Defenders of Home*. Ed. Lisa M. DeTora. Jefferson, NC: McFarland, 2009. 61–76.

Mirzoeff, Nicholas. *Bodyscape: Art, Modernity and the Ideal Figure*. London: Routledge, 1995.

Mori, Masahiro. "The Uncanny Valley." 1970. Trans. Karl F. MacDorman and Norri Kageki. *IEEE Spectrum*. June 12, 2012. www.spectrum.ieee.org/automaton/robotics/humanoids/the-uncanny-valley. Accessed Oct. 10, 2014. Web.

Nems, Mark. 2014. "Robby the Robot Filmography." http://www.nemsworld.com/robby/. Accessed Feb. 10, 2014. Web.

Nocks, Lisa. *The Robot: The Life Story of a Technology*. Westport, CT: Greenwood, 2008.

Palmer, Lorrie. "She's Just a Girl: A Cyborg Passes in *The Sarah Connor Chronicles*." *Science Fiction Film, Television, and Adaptation: Across the Screens*. Eds. J. P. Telotte and Gerald Duchovnay. New York: Routledge, 2012. 84–98.

Pierson, Michele. *Special Effects: Still in Search of Wonder*. New York: Columbia UP, 2002.

Postman, Neil. *Amusing Ourselves to Death: Public Discourse in the Age of Show Business*. New York: Viking Penguin, 1985.

Quirk, Lawrence J., and William Schoell. *Joan Crawford: The Essential Biography*. Lexington: UP of Kentucky, 2002.

Richardson, Jeffrey. "Cowboys and Robots: The Birth of the Science Fiction Western." *Crossed Genres*. Apr. 26, 2009. www.crossedgenres.com/archives/006/cowboys-and-robots-by-jeffrey-richardson. Accessed October 16, 2013. Web.

Roberts, Adam. *The History of Science Fiction*. New York: Palgrave MacMillan, 2005.

Romanyshyn, Robert D. *Technology as Symptom and Dream*. London: Routledge, 1989.

Schelde, Per. *Androids, Humanoids, and Other Science Fiction Monsters: Science and Soul in Science Fiction Film*. New York: New York UP, 1993.

Schwartz, Richard A. *Cold War Culture: Media and the Arts, 1945–1990*. New York: Checkmark, 2000.

Segal, Howard P. *Future Imperfect: The Mixed Blessings of Technology in America*. Amherst: University of Massachusetts P, 1994.

Sobchack, Vivian. "Images of Wonder: The Look of Science Fiction." *Liquid Metal: The Science Fiction Film Reader*. Ed. Sean Redmond. London: Wallflower Press, 2004. 4–10.

Sontag, Susan. "The Imagination of Disaster." *Against Interpretation*. New York: Dell, 1966. 212–28.

———. "Notes on 'Camp.'" *Against Interpretation*. New York: Dell, 1966. 277–93.

St. Pierre, Paul Matthew. *Music Hall Mimesis in British Film, 1895–1960: On the Halls on the Screen*. Madison, NJ: Fairleigh Dickinson UP, 2009.

Stewart, Garrett. "The 'Videology' of Science Fiction." *Shadows of the Magic Lamp: Fantasy and Science Fiction in Film*. Ed. George E. Slusser and Eric S. Rabkin. Carbondale: Southern Illinois UP, 1985. 159–207.

Suvin, Darko. *Metamorphoses of Science Fiction*. New Haven: Yale UP, 1979.

Tanner, Ron. "Mr. Atomic, Mr. Mercury, and Chime Trooper: Japan's Answer to the American Dream." *Asian Popular Culture*. Ed. John A. Lent. Boulder, CO: Westview Press, 1995. 79–102.

Telotte, J. P. *Replications: A Robotic History of the Science Fiction Film*. Urbana: University of Illinois P, 1995.

———. "Sex and Machines: The 'Buzz' of 1950s Science Fiction Films." *Science Fiction Film and Television* 8: 3 (2015): 371–86.

———, and Gerald Duchovnay, eds. *Science Fiction Film, Television, and Adaptation: Across the Screens*: London: Routledge, 2013.

Thomas, Bob. *Joan Crawford: A Biography*. New York: Simon and Schuster, 1978.

Todorov, Tzvetan. *The Fantastic: A Structural Approach to a Literary Genre*. Trans. Richard Howard. Ithaca, NY: Cornell UP, 1975.

Tuska, Jon. *The Vanishing Legion: A History of Mascot Pictures, 1927–1935*. Jefferson, NC: McFarland, 1982.

Vanne, Chris D. "Action Figures of Cameron in TSCC." *Summer-Glau.com*. Nov. 11, 2011. www.summer-glau.com/blog/actions_figures_of_cameron_in_tscc/2011-11-11-180. Accessed June 24, 2015. Web.

Virilio, Paul. *The Art of the Motor*. Trans. Julie Rose. Bloomington: Indiana UP, 1994.

———. *The Lost Dimension*. Trans. Daniel Moshenberg. New York: Sermiotext(e), 1991.

———. *The Vision Machine*. Trans. Julie Rose. "Bloomington: Indiana UP, 1994.

"What Is It?" *The Sketch* 39 (Oct. 15, 1902): 511, 527.

Wilson, Richard Guy. "America and the Machine Age." *The Machine Age in America: 1918–1941*. Ed. Richard Guy Wilson, Dianne H. Pilgrim, and Dickran Tashjian. New York: Abrams, 1986. 23–41.

Young, James E. "How to Manage Robots and People Working Together." *The Wall Street Journal*. June 2, 2015. www.wsj.com/articles/how-to-manage-robots-and-people-working-together-1433301051. Accessed June 28, 2015. Web.

Young, Mark S., Steve Dain, Miles Richardson, and Harlan Ellison. *Blast Off: Rockets, Robots, Ray Guns, and Rarities from the Golden Age of Space Toys*. Victoria, Canada: Dark Horse Books, 2001.

Index